Atlantic
Security

Atlantic
Security

Contending Visions

CHARLES A. KUPCHAN
Editor

A Council on Foreign Relations Book

The Council on Foreign Relations, a nonprofit, nonpartisan national membership organization founded in 1921, is dedicated to promoting understanding of international affairs through the free and civil exchange of ideas. The Council's members are dedicated to the belief that America's peace and prosperity are firmly linked to that of the world. From this flows the mission of the Council: to foster America's understanding of its fellow members of the international community, near and far, their peoples, cultures, histories, hopes, quarrels, and ambitions; and thus to serve, protect, and advance America's own global interests through study and debate, private and public.

THE COUNCIL TAKES NO INSTITUTIONAL POSITION ON POLICY ISSUES AND HAS NO AFFILIATION WITH THE U.S. GOVERNMENT. ALL STATEMENTS OF FACT AND EXPRESSIONS OF OPINION CONTAINED IN ALL ITS PUBLICATIONS ARE THE SOLE RESPONSIBILITY OF THE AUTHOR OR AUTHORS.

Council on Foreign Relations Books are distributed by Brookings Institution Press (1-800-275-1447). For further information on Council publications, please write the Council on Foreign Relations, 58 East 68th Street, New York, NY 10021, or call the Director of Communications at 212-434-9400. Or visit our website, www.foreignrelations.org.

Library of Congress Cataloging-in-Publication data

Atlantic security : contending visions / [edited by] Charles A. Kupchan.
    p. cm.
Includes bibliographical references.

   ISBN 0-87609-235-0 (pbk. : alk. paper)
   1. National security—Europe. 2. Europe—Politics and government—
1989– 3. National security—North America. I. Kupchan, Charles.

UA646 .A854   1998   98-40075
355'.03304–ddc21   CIP

9 8 7 6 5 4 3 2 1

The paper used in this publication meets the minimum requirements of the American National Standard for Information Sciences—Permanence of Paper for Printed Library Materials, ANSI Z39.48-1984

Typeset in Palatino

Composition by Cynthia Stock
Silver Spring, Maryland

Printed by Edwards Brothers
Lillington, North Carolina

Foreword

MANY OF the certainties that cemented U.S.-European security ties during the Cold War have given way to fundamental questions about the future character of the Western Alliance. Where is the transatlantic security relationship headed? What vision should shape upcoming decisions about future waves of NATO enlargement, about Russia's relationship with the West, and about the balance of responsibility between Europe and America in managing European security? How are domestic politics within the Western democracies likely to affect security relations among them? These basic questions will confront leaders in the United States and Europe as they work through the agenda of transatlantic partnership.

The authors in this volume step back from ongoing policy debates to provide three competing visions of how best to ensure peace and stability within the Atlantic community. Each author grounds his analysis in a different theoretical tradition. Accordingly, the volume speaks both to those interested in policy analysis as well as those seeking to understand competing intellectual paradigms and the insights they offer in understanding the evolving international landscape. Kupchan, Walt, and Wæver succeed in making a contribution not just to the study of transatlantic relations, but also to the architecture of the new international system that is emerging as the next century opens.

This book is one of three volumes to emerge from the Council's W. Averell Harriman Study Group on transatlantic relations. The other two volumes are *Transatlantic Economic Relations in the Post–Cold War Era*, edited by Barry Eichengreen, and *Centralization or Fragmentation? Europe Facing the Challenges of Deepening, Diversity, and Democracy*, edited by Andrew Moravcsik.

Gary C. Hufbauer
Maurice R. Greenberg Chair, Director of Studies
Council on Foreign Relations

Acknowledgments

Previous drafts of the chapters in this volume were presented at the Council on Foreign Relations in the W. Averell Harriman Study Group on Transatlantic Relations. I would like to thank the participants of the study group as well as its chairman, Roger Altman, for their thoughtful comments. Nicholas Rizopoulos provided editorial advice and wise counsel on matters of substance. For research assistance, I would like to thank Delphine Park and Mark Patton.

Contents

Chapter 1

Introduction

Charles A. Kupchan

THE TRANSATLANTIC COMMUNITY has been the anchor of global stability since World War II. The partnership of North American and European democracies enabled capitalism and democracy to triumph over Soviet communism. Since the collapse of the Soviet empire, these democracies have continued to work together to enlarge the zone of democratic peace and to deepen and broaden an open international trading order.

Although policymakers and scholars alike agree that the next century will be a more peaceful one if the transatlantic link remains vital, they also agree that this goal will be difficult to achieve. No imminent outside threat binds North America and Europe. The community of Atlantic democracies is growing in size, complicating the task of forging a common response to challenges. Social and economic problems within their own countries will curtail the interest of electorates in problems beyond their borders. And a volatile combination of economic turmoil and geopolitical competition in East Asia could draw America's attention away from the Atlantic to the Pacific.

Where is the transatlantic security relationship headed? Is it worth preserving? Is it possible to preserve it and, if so, how? What are the main challenges to the viability of the transatlantic community, and how can they be overcome?

This volume addresses these questions by juxtaposing three essays grounded in competing theoretical traditions. My goal in commissioning articles from authors working in different traditions was not just to enliven the book by pitting rival analytic perspectives against each other;

1

I also wanted to deepen the ongoing debate over U.S.-European relations by clarifying the intellectual roots of this debate and uncovering the different starting points that inform alternative policy choices.

All too often discussions of transatlantic relations become mired in arguments over the merits of NATO enlargement or of European monetary union. Lost in the debate is a proper consideration of the competing conceptual foundations of different policy positions. Because the present historical period is one of great fluidity and unpredictability, basing policy on solid conceptual foundations is especially important. Inasmuch as this volume lays out competing theoretical perspectives and traces their policy implications, it should be of considerable use to both students interested in mapping the intellectual landscape and policymakers looking for their bearings in an era of profound change.

This book thus seeks to fill a particular niche. It focuses on competing visions of Atlantic security and lays out alternative paths for the long term, not discrete policy options for the near term. NATO enlargement is moving ahead. The outlines of the policies and of the strategic landscape that will emerge in the next few years are becoming clear. But the hardest and most important questions loom on the horizon. What comes after the first wave of NATO enlargement? How far east should Europe extend? Can and should America remain a European power? These questions are central to shaping where the Atlantic community should head and what overarching vision it should seek to bring to fruition. It is essential to lay out and evaluate these contending visions now, for only by doing so can Europe and North America increase the likelihood of arriving at a desired endpoint.

Three analytic positions are represented in this volume. Stephen Walt's chapter presents a realist account of transatlantic relations. Walt considers the international system anarchic and competitive, and national states are its key constituent units. From this perspective, the end of the cold war does not augur well for the transatlantic relationship on three counts. First, the absence of a common external threat will weaken the bond between North America and western Europe. Second, the transition from bipolarity to multipolarity will produce a less stable and less predictable international environment. Finally, national states will become harder to govern and their electorates more focused on domestic problems, limiting the scope of their foreign engagement. The transatlantic community can do little to overcome such powerful structural determinants. Walt's main admonition is that its members should lower their expectations and prepare for a transatlantic link that enjoys neither the prominence nor the cohesion of recent decades.

Ole Wæver's point of departure is at the other end of the analytic spectrum. In his view the international system is not characterized by anarchy nor are national states its key constituent units. On the contrary, both the international system and the units that compose it are socially and politically constructed. Dynamics within the international system are not predetermined by some objective measure of structure or polarity; they are determined by the willful agency of the units that make up the system. Through believing that they share a common political space and acting as if they do, Europe's national states have entered a post-sovereign era. The European Union (EU) no longer consists of independent nation-states each concerned about its own welfare. Instead, it is a neoimperial political construction, with the Franco-German coalition at its core and other members arraying themselves in concentric circles around this power center. Europe is not moving toward multipolarity, but toward unipolarity.

For Wæver, the key challenge that lies ahead is moving forward with the integration of Europe and creating an identity for Europe that is consonant with and ultimately subsumes Europe's separate national identities—particularly those in France and Germany. Stability on the continent rests on sustaining the process of unification and the establishment of Europe as an independent global actor. Inasmuch as America's presence in Europe continues to facilitate integration and buys time for the EU to mature and ultimately to manage its own security, a continuation of the transatlantic link serves an important function. But the U.S.-European tie is not an end in itself; it is a means to the end of furthering the enterprise of European integration.

My own analysis rests on the middle ground between Walt and Wæver. Like Walt, I believe that material power matters a great deal in international politics, that the national state is alive and well, and that the international system provides strong incentives for competitive behavior among the states that compose it. But like Wæver, I take seriously the notion of national identity and believe that states have character. The identity and character of states have a powerful effect on their behavior and, accordingly, on the international dynamics associated with the distribution of material resources. In this sense, my position represents a synthesis of realism and constructivism.

In more concrete terms, the democratic states of the West have succeeded in carving out a pocket of nonanarchic space, a community in which trust and expectations of reciprocity as well as a shared identity overcome the incentives for national competition and rivalry. Both institutionalist and constructivist paradigms provide insight into how this nonanarchic space evolves. From an institutionalist perspective, repeated interaction and the proliferation of rule-based institutions have facilitated cooperation and mutual trust. From a constructivist perspective, the character and identity of the Western states have converged, and their shared commitment to capitalist and democratic values has deepened. As a result of both processes, war among the members of this community has become virtually unthinkable. Because the members of this community identify each other as partners rather than competitors, a multipolar structure that has the potential to heighten competition does not do so. States believe that one another's power will be used to benign ends. Trust and shared identity thus overwhelm polarity and avert anarchy, erecting in its place a nascent society of states.

The challenge for the future is, from this perspective, to lock in and gradually enlarge this community of liberal democracies among which war has become unthinkable. Doing so entails nurturing a shared identity that enables the national state and a supranational union of those states to coexist comfortably. The purpose of union is to moderate and bind power, not, as in Wæver's conception, to amass it. Instead of working toward a European Union that becomes a global actor, the Western democracies should seek to establish an Atlantic union that consolidates their nonwar community. Such a union of Atlantic democracies needs to find a balance between an institutional design that demands too much from member states, and is therefore politically unsustainable, and a formulation that is so limited in its effects that the transatlantic community is left to unravel and revert to the more austere world described by Walt. The creation of a nonanarchic space that spans North America and western Europe is a revolutionary development. Scholars and policymakers alike need to think hard about how to preserve it.

Chapter 2

The Precarious Partnership
America and Europe in a New Era

Stephen M. Walt

POLITICIANS on both sides of the Atlantic are fond of describing the North Atlantic Treaty Organization (NATO) as the most successful military alliance in modern history. Who can blame them? The transatlantic partnership between Europe and America brought peace to a war-torn continent, overcame the Soviet challenge, and provided a safe haven in which to nurture European political and economic integration. Security ties between Europe and America also facilitated cooperation on a variety of other issues, helping to foster a remarkable period of material prosperity.[1]

Given these achievements, it is hardly surprising that few voices now call for an end to the alliance, even though its original raison d'être has evaporated. If anything, support for NATO seems more widespread than ever, and the member states have now invited Poland, Hungary, and Czechoslovakia to begin negotiations for accession. NATO has developed a new strategic concept to guide its force planning in the post–cold war era and revised its doctrinal procedures and institutional arrangements to reflect the momentous changes that have occurred since 1989.[2]

---

1. These dynamics are stressed in Josef Joffe, "Europe's American Pacifier," *Foreign Policy*, vol. 54 (Spring 1984); Josef Joffe, *The Limited Partnership: Europe, the United States, and the Burdens of Alliance* (Cambridge: Ballinger, 1987); A. W. DePorte, *Europe between the Superpowers: The Enduring Balance* (Yale University Press, 1979); and Joanne Gowa, *Allies, Adversaries, and International Trade* (Princeton University Press, 1994).

2. The new "strategic concept" adopted in 1991 deemphasizes forward defense and

After an embarrassing period of disagreement and vacillation, NATO helped bring the bloody war in Bosnia to an end (at least temporarily), in the process reaffirming the U.S. commitment to Europe and underscoring the alliance's continued relevance in the post–cold war world. At first glance, therefore, the transatlantic partnership seems to be confounding the widespread belief that alliances invariably dissolve once the threat that brought them together is gone.[3]

Unfortunately, these developments mask a more troubling reality. Public declarations of commitment provide unreliable evidence of common purpose, and the more fervent and frequent these declarations, the greater the possibility that they are actually signs of doubt.[4] Thus Senator Richard Lugar declared that "NATO must go out-of-area or go out of business," and former NATO secretary-general Manfred Wörner repeatedly stressed the need to broaden NATO's mission in order to ensure its continued relevance.[5] Similarly, Christoph Bertram has warned that "left to itself, the sense of shared destiny that still, in a lingering sort of way, holds Europe and America together is bound to disappear."[6] The Clinton administration's decision to commit U.S. troops in Bosnia was hardly an unambiguous sign of NATO's continued health, given that the decision was inspired in part by the belief that failure to act would have a cata-

---

nuclear weapons and relies on new "rapid reaction forces" to deal with lesser contingencies. NATO leaders have also begun to revise the alliance's command structure to reflect these new concerns, as exemplified by the January 1994 decision endorsing the concept of combined joint task forces (CJTFs) to meet a wider range of non-Article 5 contingencies. See Simon Duke, *The New European Security Disorder* (New York: St. Martin's, 1994), pp. 288–94; and Charles Barry, "NATO's Combined Joint Task Forces in Theory and Practice," *Survival*, vol. 38, no. 1 (1996), pp. 81–97.

3. See Robert B. McCalla, "NATO's Persistence after the Cold War," *International Organization*, vol. 50, no. 3 (1996).

4. As Ronald D. Asmus notes, "If one looks beyond the proclamations of unity and success presented by transatlantic officialdom, there is far less certainty, let alone agreement, about the future purpose or function of the transatlantic partnership." See his "Redefining the Atlantic Partnership after the Cold War," in David Gompert and F. Stephen Larrabee, eds., *America and Europe* (Cambridge: Cambridge University Press, 1997), p. 20.

5. Senator Lugar's remarks to the Overseas Writers Club, 23 June 1993, and also Manfred Wörner, "A Vigorous Alliance: A Motor for Peaceful Change in Europe," *NATO Review*, vol. 40, no. 6 (1992).

6. Christoph Bertram, *Europe in the Balance: Securing the Peace Won in the Cold War* (Washington, D.C.: Carnegie Endowment for International Peace, 1995), p. 87. Bertram notes that "the fear of Soviet power pressed Western Europe and the United States into a cohesive form for half a century," but he also warns that "the appearance of cohesion will be short-lived" now that the Soviet threat is gone.

strophic effect on transatlantic solidarity.[7] Finally, the recent decision to expand NATO seems to have been motivated as much by the fear that the alliance will fade into irrelevance as by confidence in its enduring value. When great powers are forced to take actions they would prefer to avoid merely to keep allies from questioning their credibility, it suggests that the relationship they are trying to sustain may not be robust.

Furthermore, although there is widespread agreement that NATO must adapt to the far-reaching changes in the international security environment, a clear consensus on the ultimate purpose of the alliance is still lacking. Some European experts have called for transforming the alliance into a "problem-solving community . . . dedicated to the advancement of civilization and stability abroad," while others have seen a revised NATO as a stepping-stone to the creation of an independent European defense identity.[8] Prominent U.S. experts have proposed a new "transatlantic bargain," whereby the United States maintains its stabilizing presence in Europe in exchange for European support in other regions, although they recognize that such a bargain would not be easy to achieve or maintain.[9] The Clinton administration sees NATO's main aim as "helping manage ethnic and national conflicts" and "extending the scope of security cooperation to the new democracies of Europe," and this basic view provides its main justification for expanding NATO eastward.[10] The case for expansion has not gone unchallenged, however,

7. According to an earlier statement by President Clinton: "As NATO's leader and the primary broker of the peace agreement, the United States must be an essential part of the mission (in Bosnia). If we're not there, NATO will not be there. . . . A conflict that already has claimed so many victims could spread like poison . . . eat away at Europe's stability and erode our partnership with our European allies." See "Clinton's Words on Bosnia: The Right Thing to Do," *New York Times*, November 28, 1995, p. A6.

8. See Werner Weidenfeld, "The Future of the Transatlantic Relationship," and Phillip Borinski, "Europe and America: Between Drift and New Order," in Alton Frye and Werner Weidenfeld, eds., *Europe and America: Between Drift and New Order* (Gutersloh: Bertelsmann Foundation, 1993); French efforts to link NATO to a new European defense identity have been especially strong. See Robert P. Grant, "France's New Relationship with NATO," *Survival*, vol. 38, no. 1 (1996), pp. 62–64.

9. See Ronald D. Asmus, Robert Blackwill, and F. Stephen Larrabee, "Can NATO Survive?" *Washington Quarterly*, vol. 19, no. 2 (1996).

10. See William J. Clinton, *A National Security Strategy of Engagement and Enlargement* (Washington, D.C.: 1995), p. 26. For arguments endorsing NATO expansion, see Henry Kissinger, "Expand NATO Now," *Washington Post*, December 19, 1994; Zbigniew Brzezinski, "A Plan for Europe," *Foreign Affairs*, vol. 74, no. 1 (1995); Strobe Talbott, "Why NATO Should Grow," *New York Review of Books*, August 10, 1995, pp. 29-30; and Ronald D. Asmus, Richard Kugler, and F. Stephen Larrabee, "Building a New NATO," *Foreign*

and other writers offer more pessimistic appraisals of NATO's long-term future.[11]

Whatever the outcome of these debates, the transatlantic partnership is at a crossroads. This chapter seeks to describe that intersection by identifying the underlying trends that will affect security relations between Europe and America in the twenty-first century. If an alliance is first and foremost an agreement for security cooperation between a group of sovereign states, then efforts to forecast its future should begin by considering the specific security problems that the various members will face as well as the constraints that will impinge on their ability to meet them.

In this chapter, I devote relatively little attention to specific policy initiatives, concentrating instead on the more enduring forces that lie beneath them. My general perspective is based on the familiar realist paradigm. I assume that states will remain the preeminent actors in world politics, and I further assume that all states seek to survive and, if possible, to prosper. Because no agency or institution can reliably protect states from one another, governments worry a lot about security and pay close attention to potential threats. International politics is thus an inherently competitive realm; present allies may be future adversaries

---

Affairs, vol. 72, no. 4 (1993). Scholarly discussions of NATO's potential role as a security management institution include McCalla, "NATO's Persistence," pp. 465–67, 471–72; and Celeste Wallander and Robert O. Keohane, "Why Does NATO Persist? An Institutionalist Approach," Harvard University, 1996, pp. 23–26.

11. Critics of NATO expansion include Michael Mandelbaum, "NATO Expansion: Bridge to the 19th Century," Occasional Paper (Chevy Chase, Md.: Center for Political and Strategic Studies, June 1997); and Michael Brown, "The Flawed Logic of NATO Expansion," *Survival,* vol. 37, no. 1 (1995). For pessimistic appraisals of NATO's future, see John J. Mearsheimer, "The Future of America's Continental Commitment," paper prepared for the Norwegian Nobel Institute's Symposium on the United States and Western Europe, Oslo, Norway, April 9–12, 1997; John J. Mearsheimer, "Back to the Future: Europe after the Cold War," *International Security,* vol. 15, no. 1 (1990); Stephen M. Walt, *The Origins of Alliances* (Cornell University Press, 1987, preface to 1990 paperback edition); and Kenneth N. Waltz, "The Emerging Structure of International Politics," *International Security,* vol. 18, no. 2 (1993), pp. 75–76. Advocates of U.S. disengagement include Earl Ravenal, *Designing Defense for a New World Order: The Military Budget in 1992 and Beyond* (Washington, D.C.: Cato Institute, 1991); Eric A. Nordlinger, *Isolationism Reconfigured: American Foreign Policy for a New Century* (Princeton University Press, 1995); and Ted Galen Carpenter, *Beyond NATO: Staying Out of Europe's Wars* (Washington, D.C.: CATO Institute, 1994). NATO's value as hedge against a resurgent Russia is stressed by Charles L. Glaser, "Why NATO Is Still Best: Future Security Arrangements for Europe," *International Security,* vol. 18, no. 1 (1993).

(and vice versa), and the danger of war is always present (albeit to widely varying degrees).[12]

Unlike some realists, however, I do not believe that the distribution of capabilities (the balance of power) is the sole or even the most important factor shaping international outcomes. Although major changes in the balance of power invariably exert profound effects on states' behavior, they do not necessarily determine how great powers will respond. States' behavior is also affected by their perceptions of other states' intentions (however uncertain such judgments may be), by geography, and by their own beliefs about the cost and benefits of alternative courses of action. Attempting to depict the future security environment thus requires us to consider both systemic and "unit-level" factors.[13]

Accordingly, Part I begins by summarizing what has not changed in international security affairs, and then examines the implications of developments occurring at what might loosely be termed the systemic level. Part II addresses changes occurring within the member states, and argues that these domestic factors will be even more important now that the confining logic of bipolarity is absent. The conclusion summarizes these results and sketches their implications. Specifically, I predict that transatlantic relations will experience growing and largely unavoidable tensions. By lowering expectations, however, the alliance can preserve its most valuable elements and minimize the risk of an abrupt and premature rupture.

The New International Environment

Before we turn to the new developments that have arisen since 1989, it is worth reminding ourselves that a number of important elements of

12. Important guides to modern realist thinking include Kenneth N. Waltz, *Theory of International Politics* (Reading, Mass.: Addison-Wesley, 1979); Robert O. Keohane, ed., *Neorealism and Its Critics* (Columbia University Press, 1986); Michael E. Brown, Sean M. Lynn-Jones, and Steven E. Miller, eds., *The Perils of Anarchy: Contemporary Realism and International Security* (MIT Press, 1995); and Benjamin Frankel, ed., *Realism: Restatements and Renewal* (London: Frank Cass, 1996).

13. My views on realism are spelled out in *The Origins of Alliances* (Cornell University Press, 1987); *Revolution and War* (Cornell University Press, 1996); "Alliances, Threats, and U.S. Grand Strategy: A Reply to Kaufman and Labs," *Security Studies*, vol. 1, no. 3 (1992); and "The Progressive Power of Realism," *American Political Science Review*, vol. 91, no. 4 (1997).

world politics have not changed. To begin with, the international system remains an anarchic order in which states are the ultimate guarantors of their (and their citizens') security. As the Kuwaitis, Bosnian Muslims, Hutu, Tutsi, and Chechens have discovered, there is still no global agency that can protect states (or peoples) from each other. Although alliances and other forms of security cooperation can enhance their members' security in a variety of ways, ultimately each state is still forced, in Thucydides's well-known phrase, to "do what it can, or suffer what it must."[14]

Second, the state remains the principal institutional form for the organization of international political life. Even in the European Union, where the process of economic and political integration is most advanced, the state's hold on individual identities and loyalties remains strong.[15] Nationalism is even more vibrant elsewhere, as evidenced by the dissolution of the former Soviet Union, the ethnic and nationalist pressures within Russia itself, the electoral triumph of the Hindu Nationalist party in India, and the persistent pressure for autonomy or independence in Quebec, Scotland, Catalonia, Kurdistan, and elsewhere. Nongovernmental organizations and substate actors may be of increasing importance in certain realms of world politics, but they have yet to pose a sustained challenge to the state either as the locus of individual identity or as the principal agency for meeting political demands. This is especially true in the realm of security affairs, where the capacity of states to use violence for political ends dwarfs the capabilities of any other actors.

Third, and following from the second point, the member states of NATO continue to regard the world as potentially dangerous, and, although some experts portray the industrial democracies as a "pluralistic security community" from which security concerns have been largely banished, recent developments suggest that this view is at best premature.[16] The collapse of the Soviet Union and the reunification of Ger-

---

14. Thucydides, *The Peloponnesian War,* ed. J. Finley (Modern Library, 1951), p. 331.

15. See Anthony Smith, "National Identity and the Idea of European Unity," *International Affairs,* vol. 68, no. 1 (1992).

16. Optimistic appraisals of the European future include Richard Ullmann, *Securing Europe* (Princeton University Press, 1991); John Mueller, *Quiet Cataclysm: Reflections on the Recent Transformation of World Politics* (HarperCollins, 1995); Max Singer and Aaron B. Wildavsky, *The Real World Order: Zones of Peace, Zones of Turmoil* (Chatham House Publishers, 1993); Daniel Deudney and G. John Ikenberry, "The Logic of the West," *World Policy Journal,* vol. 10, no. 4 (1993–94); Robert Jervis, "The Future of World Politics: Will It Resemble the Past?" *International Security,* vol. 16, no. 3 (1991–92); Stephen Van Evera,

many rekindled familiar concerns about the balance of power in Europe, and European elites are clearly worried that security competition could reemerge.[17] Europe and America have acted skillfully to dampen such fears, but that does not mean that they are not present.[18]

Fourth, modern warfare remains extraordinarily destructive. Not only are the strongest powers increasingly able to sow damage and death at very great distances, but the spread of modern small arms and other conventional munitions now permits relatively undeveloped societies to wreak fearsome havoc on their neighbors (or on beleaguered minorities within their borders).[19] Even if forecasts of an imminent "revolution in military affairs" are accurate, modern war will not become less lethal.[20] Quite the contrary. Improvements in target acquisition and guidance may allow the most advanced states to reduce the level of collateral damage they inflict, but the net effect of these technological developments will be an increase in battlefield lethality. And if the 1991 Gulf War suggests that great powers may be able to take on weaker states with near impunity (at least under certain conditions), a great power conflict under modern conditions would almost certainly be an extraordinarily costly and bloody affair. Even if we omit the awesome capaci-

---

"Primed for Peace: Europe after the Cold War," *International Security*, vol. 15, no. 3 (1990–91); and Michael Mandelbaum, *The Dawn of Peace in Europe* (New York: Twentieth Century Fund, 1996). The phrase "pluralistic security community" is taken from Karl Deutsch and others, *Political Community in the North Atlantic Area: International Organization in Light of Historical Experience* (Princeton University Press, 1957).

17. Thus Czech president Vaclav Havel warned that if NATO fails to expand, "We could be heading for a new global catastrophe . . . [which] could cost us all much more than the two world wars," and Christoph Bertram has argued, "To disband NATO now would throw Europe into deep insecurity. . . . It would threaten political stability in the newly democratic states of Eastern Europe and political cohesion among the integrated states of Western Europe. For both Europe and the United States, it would be a strategic disaster." See Bertram, *Europe in the Balance*, pp. 17–18. Needless to say, these are not the words of men who believe that great-power competition has been forever banished from Europe.

18. See in particular Robert J. Art, "Why Europe Needs the United States and NATO," *Political Science Quarterly*, vol. 111, no. 1 (1996). The fear of renewed security competition does not mean that NATO's members presently regard one another as rivals, only that they recognize the *potential* for rivalry should interests conflict.

19. The long and bloody conflict between Iran and Iraq is an obvious example, as are the recent war between Azerbaijan and Armenia and the bitter, bloody civil wars in Sri Lanka, Sudan, Tadzhikistan, Yugoslavia, and Rwanda.

20. For an accessible introduction to these issues, see Eliot A. Cohen, "A Revolution in Warfare," *Foreign Affairs*, vol. 75, no. 2 (1996).

ties of nuclear weapons, modern industrial warfare will remain extremely costly for the foreseeable future.

A related phenomenon is the declining benefit of territorial conquest. As the costs of war have risen and the potential gains from trade have increased, the net benefits of expansion have declined significantly. The spread of nationalism has made it harder for foreign occupiers to subdue restive local populations (especially in areas where guerrilla war is a viable means of resistance), and the diffusion of conventional weaponry and military expertise has reinforced this trend. The emergence of postindustrial economies may have decreased the value of occupation even more, because such economies depend on free flows of information that are at least somewhat corrosive to authoritarian rule. Wars may still arise from ideological motives or from insecurity, but they are less likely to be motivated by simple material greed.[21]

The high cost of war and the declining benefit of conquest do not imply that military matters and security questions are of declining relevance, however. If anything, they suggest that these issues have become even more important because the consequences of error are more severe. Moreover, the high costs of war and the declining benefits of conquest are not immutable features of nature, and national leaders have demonstrated ample capacity to misread them in the past. What is needed, therefore, is a clear-eyed appraisal of how these enduring features of world politics will interact with the new circumstances that the great powers now face.

At the systemic level, the new security environment is characterized by three interrelated developments: the reemergence of multipolarity; the globalization of economic and social processes; and the transformation of the security agenda.

Multipolarity

It is commonplace to acknowledge that the collapse of the Soviet Union has eliminated the principal glue that held NATO together for forty years.

---

21. These arguments are drawn from Van Evera, "Primed for Peace"; Jervis, "Future of World Politics," and Robert Jervis, "A Usable Past for the Future," in Michael Hogan, ed., *The End of the Cold War: Its Meanings and Implications* (Cambridge University Press, 1995). For an important contrasting view, see Peter Liberman, "The Spoils of Conquest," *International Security*, vol. 8, no. 2 (1993); and Peter Liberman, *Does Conquest Pay? The Exploitation of Occupied Industrial Societies* (Princeton University Press, 1996).

Less frequently heard is a careful consideration of what a return to a world of several great powers will mean.[22] Structural changes exert far-reaching effects that are often difficult to anticipate because they alter the entire setting in which the major players interact. Options that were previously unfeasible become possible; ambitions that remained unspoken are now openly proclaimed; and problems that were previously ignored loom larger.[23] Because each state's strategy depends on what the others will do, a change in the number of major players will alter the problems each perceives, the goals that each seeks, and the means they use to achieve them.[24]

What will the new structure of world politics look like? At present, and for the foreseeable future, the United States will be first among equals among the great powers. Its gross domestic product still outstrips the other major powers, and only complete European unification or the unlikely event of China's sustaining its present growth rates will threaten U.S. economic primacy much before the year 2020. Below the United States, the other great economic powers include China, Japan, and Germany, with France, Great Britain, Russia, and possibly India trailing behind, depending on the evolution of economic and political trends in the latter two states.[25]

22. For theoretical discussions of the differences between bipolar and multipolar systems, see Waltz, *Theory of International Politics*; and Glenn Snyder and Paul Diesing, *Conflict among Nations: Bargaining, Decisionmaking, and System Structure in International Crises* (Princeton University Press, 1977), pp. 419–29. Recent efforts to trace these effects in the post–cold war world (reaching a variety of conclusions) include Mearsheimer, "Back to the Future"; Van Evera, "Primed for Peace"; Waltz, "The Emerging Structure"; Charles Kegley and Gregory A. Raymond, *A Multipolar Peace? Great Power Politics in the 21st Century* (New York: St. Martin's, 1994); and Christopher Mark Davis, "War and Peace in a Multipolar World: A Critique of Quincy Wright's Institutional Analysis of the Interwar International System," *Journal of Strategic Studies*, vol. 19, no. 1 (1996).

23. For example, the contemporary debate on the future course of German foreign policy is more diverse than at any time since the early 1950s. See Gunther Hellman, "Goodbye Bismarck? The Foreign Policy of Contemporary Germany," *Mershon International Studies Review*, vol. 40, no. 1 (1996).

24. Structural changes also permit actors to pursue goals that they did not even consider previously. For example, an outside observer would learn little about my interest in owning a Mercedes-Benz from either my past decisions or my verbal statements because the option lies far outside the realm of possibility and I rarely even think about it. Were I to win a lottery jackpot, however, I might suddenly discover a desire—or even the "need"—for a Mercedes-Benz, contrary to all the earlier evidence.

25. A useful corrective to alarmist speculation about Asian economic growth is Paul Krugman, "The Myth of Asia's Miracle," *Foreign Affairs*, vol. 73, no. 6 (1994).

14   Stephen M. Walt

The United States will also remain the world's leading military power unless a cost-conscious electorate dismantles the cold war military establishment far more extensively than it has to date. U.S. defense spending is currently more than three times greater than that of Russia, five or six times greater than that of Japan or Germany (the third and fourth powers as of 1995), and roughly nine times greater than that of China.[26] Even if U.S. military power does decline, most of the other major powers are reducing their arsenals nearly as fast.[27] Only China is presently engaged in a significant military buildup, and it has a long way to go.

Thus the world of the early twenty-first century will be inhabited by several great powers, with the United States clearly the strongest both economically and militarily. Multipolarity at the global level will increase the relative importance of regional forces because there will no longer be a bipolar rivalry driving both superpowers to meddle in every corner of the globe. Indeed, the dismantling of cold war military establishments will make it more difficult for any of the great powers to engage in extensive military operations—particularly outside their own regions—simply because they will lack the manpower, weaponry, and mobility assets. Thus the 1991 Gulf war, which was fought with the resources and expertise amassed over four decades of cold war competition, may have been a last vestige of the bipolar past rather than a harbinger of the multipolar future.

How will the return to multipolarity affect transatlantic security relations? At least five main effects are likely.

THE DECLINING CONGRUENCE OF INTERESTS. Although NATO's member states never agreed on everything, the rigid logic of bipolarity pro-

26. In light of Russian president Boris Yeltsin's plans to further reduce Russian defense expenditures, the gap between the United States and Russia is virtually certain to grow. Estimates of Chinese defense spending vary widely, but even the highest estimates place it at roughly a fifth of the U.S. total. See "Defence Expenditures of NATO Countries, 1975–1995," *NATO Review* (January 1996), pp. 31–33; *The Military Balance 1995–96* (London: International Institute for Strategic Studies, 1995), pp. 263–67, 270–75; and *The Military Balance 1996–97* (London: International Institute for Strategic Studies, 1996), pp. 306–11.

27. Between 1990 and 1995, U.S. defense spending declined an average of 5.3 percent a year. German defense spending declined an average of 7.2 percent a year from 1990 to 1994, British spending declined 4.3 percent, and French spending 0.9 percent. German spending recently increased slightly, but the French announced even more dramatic cuts in 1996. Russian defense spending is perhaps a third of the former Soviet total. See "Defence Expenditures of NATO Countries" and *The Military Balance 1996–97*.

vided a solid core of consensus around which to base their association.[28] Western Europe and the United States were brought together by a combination of forces, including the Soviet Union's sheer size, its geographic proximity to Europe, its large, offensively oriented military forces, and its open commitment to spreading world revolution. Because the Europeans were loath to sacrifice their independence and the United States was loath to let any single power dominate the industrial power of the Eurasian land mass, the industrial democracies of Europe and North America had ample reason to downplay their differences in order to preserve a common front.[29]

The disappearance of the Soviet threat has eliminated this overriding common interest, and though these states still possess common objectives in other realms (such as maintaining a stable global economic order and limiting the spread of nuclear weapons), these objectives are not as salient as was containing the Soviet Union. The European powers have far less need for U.S. protection, which means that their ability to make independent decisions is growing. Similarly, the United States has less need to provide security and stability for Europe in the absence of a rival superpower. Historically the United States has maintained a continental commitment in Europe only when a single power threatened to establish itself as a regional hegemon; whenever such a threat was absent, so was the United States.[30]

No two states have completely compatible interests, of course, which is why conflicts of interest are inevitable. These conflicts may be sup-

28. We should not forget that NATO's history has always been somewhat turbulent. Greece and Turkey have been at swords' points over Cyprus, and the United States and Europe clashed over Suez, Skybolt, the Euromissiles, and the Arab-Israeli conflict. With hindsight, however, it is clear that intra-alliance squabbles (including the French withdrawal in 1967) were possible in part because NATO's members had so many other interests in common. Thus disputes could strain but not threaten the basic security commitment. See Philip Gordon, "Recasting the Atlantic Alliance," *Survival*, 38, no. 1 (1996), which addresses many of the same themes as this chapter and reaches similar conclusions.

29. See Stephen M. Walt, *The Origins of Alliances* (Cornell University Press, 1987), especially chap. 8.

30. The United States intervened in World Wars I and II only when Germany seemed likely to establish regional hegemony in Europe. Because Western Europe was too weak to withstand the Soviet Union after World War II, we reluctantly agreed to maintain troops there following the formation of NATO, a commitment that eventually became semipermanent. The question is whether the U.S. presence will continue now that the danger of an emerging regional hegemon is remote. On this point, see Mearsheimer, "Future of America's Continental Commitment."

pressed when two or more states face a common threat, and alliance members usually have to compromise on some issues so as to preserve the relations that count. Moreover, alliance partners tend to be less concerned about the distribution of any gains from cooperation, both because they worry less about threats from their partners and because enhancing their allies' capabilities contributes to their own security.[31]

In the absence of a common threat, however, conflicts of interest within the alliance can be pursued with greater vigor.[32] The absence of a clear unifying threat will allow conflicts of interest to flourish, thereby undermining the atmosphere of trust and accommodation that helped the alliance weather earlier periods of disagreement. In addition to making interalliance consensus more elusive, these disputes will also affect how the different populations view each other. It will be difficult to retain a feeling of solidarity toward countries whose governments are constantly wrangling with one's own, and membership in the alliance could even become a political liability if these disputes persist. Thus, by removing the main glue that kept conflicts of interest within bounds, the end of the cold war threatens the very foundations of the Atlantic community.[33]

The logic of this argument has led some scholars to anticipate a rapid return to traditional patterns of great-power competition in Europe.[34] As discussed below, these analyses overlook or downplay a number of more encouraging developments, and the conclusions they reach are too gloomy. Nonetheless, the level of conflict within Europe and across the

31. See Gowa, *Allies, Adversaries and International Trade*; and Joanne Gowa and Edward Mansfield, "Power Politics and International Trade," *American Political Science Review*, vol. 87, no. 2 (1993).

32. Thus U.S. allies have defied the provisions of the Helms-Burton Act, which imposes sanctions on foreign companies that trade with Cuba, while complaining bitterly about high-handed U.S. policies. As Canadian minister of foreign affairs Lloyd Axworthy commented, "This is bullying. But in America, you call it global leadership." Similarly, U.S. efforts to punish European firms for trading with Iran led French prime minister Lionel Jospin to retort that "no one accepts the idea that Americans can make laws that apply on a global scale." See "Talk Multilaterally, Hit Allies with Stick," *New York Times*, July 21, 1996, p. E3; and "Bashing America for Fun and Profit," *New York Times*, October 5, 1997, pp. 4:1, 16.

33. It is worth noting that Karl Deutsch's seminal work on "pluralistic security communities" focused on the internal processes within such communities and downplayed the role of external threats in creating and sustaining harmony within them. See Deutsch and others, *Political Community in the North Atlantic Area*, especially pp. 44–46.

34. See Mearsheimer, "Back to the Future."

Atlantic is going to increase, and maintaining cohesion and consensus within the alliance will be much more difficult.[35]

THE QUESTION OF CREDIBILITY. The declining congruence of interests will exacerbate the familiar issue of credibility. Convincing the Europeans that the United States was in fact committed to their defense was a recurring problem throughout the cold war, and it led both to sensible policies like the permanent deployment of U.S. troops and more problematic actions like the Vietnam War in the 1960s or the deployment of intermediate-range nuclear forces in the 1980s.[36] In retrospect, concern for U.S. credibility was probably exaggerated because the logic of bipolarity gave the United States a profound and immediate stake in Europe's fate. So long as Soviet forces stood on the Elbe, the United States had an obvious interest in keeping western Europe independent of Soviet control. Although it was occasionally necessary to signal our continued commitment, what made these signals credible was the underlying U.S. interest in European independence.

Now that the Soviet threat is gone, however, the U.S. interest in European security has shifted from a first-order fear that Europe might be conquered to a second-order concern for preserving European stability. During the cold war, Americans saw a Soviet invasion of Europe as a direct threat to their own safety; now they see the reemergence of security competition in Europe as an event that might affect U.S. security at some point in the future. Such an event is clearly undesirable, but linking it to vital U.S. interests requires a more extended chain of reasoning. The United States and Europe are separated by geography, language, historical experience, and relative capabilities, and the U.S. interest in Europe is neither as obvious nor as significant now that there is no potential hegemon perched on NATO's doorstep.[37]

---

35. For a theoretical discussion of the forces that shape alliance cohesion, see Stephen M. Walt, "Why Alliances Endure or Collapse," *Survival*, vol. 39, no. 1 (1997).

36. Concern for the credibility of U.S. commitments was a central obsession of U.S. policymakers throughout the cold war. See especially Patrick Morgan, "Saving Face for the Sake of Deterrence," in Robert Jervis, Richard Ned Lebow, and Janice Stein, eds., *Psychology and Deterrence* (Johns Hopkins University Press, 1985). For critiques, see Walt, *Origins of Alliances*, chaps. 2 and 5; Ted Hopf, *Peripheral Visions: Deterrence Theory and American Foreign Policy in the Third World* (University of Michigan Press, 1994); and Jonathan Mercer, *Reputation and International Politics* (Cornell University Press, 1996).

37. Among other things, policymakers who are fond of proclaiming that "America is a European country" need to spend a few minutes looking at a globe. America is many things, but it is quite clearly *not* located in Europe.

Thus, no matter how often or how eloquently the president or his senior advisors reaffirm the U.S. commitment, Europeans have ample reason to doubt it. It can hardly be reassuring, for example, that the U.S. entry into Bosnia was accompanied by open hand wringing in Congress and by repeated reminders that our involvement would be of limited duration. The Bosnian episode illustrates how the United States may be forced to do more to persuade its allies of its fidelity now that its objective interest in their fate has declined. This is a dangerous paradox, however, because doing more even as one's interest declines is likely to trigger domestic resentments, thereby further jeopardizing the commitment.[38]

Ironically, doubts about the U.S. commitment may have enhanced U.S. leverage within the alliance, as fears of a complete U.S. withdrawal tend to encourage its European partners to make concessions in order to keep the Americans in. But these same doubts could also lead the Europeans to discount U.S. participation and to disregard U.S. preferences even more. Such a policy would probably hasten a U.S. withdrawal because Washington is unlikely to accept a subordinate role.

THE ABSENCE OF CLEAR BOUNDARIES. The reemergence of multipolarity also creates greater uncertainty about the proper geographic focus for the alliance itself. Under bipolarity, the iron curtain formed the central boundary on which the alliance rightly focused its attention. Although the two superpowers competed around the world, America's European partners generally remained above the global fray. And if the flanks and the various out-of area problems were neither irrelevant nor ignored, they generally received less attention than the central front.

In the post–cold war order, however, the proper geographic focus for the alliance is much less clear. This development was acknowledged at the 1991–92 Rome and Oslo summits, whose declarations spoke of "multi-faceted and multi-directional" threats and offered vague commitments to "Allied consultation" on out-of-area issues.[39] Unfortunately, the member states do not share the same geostrategic perspectives. For Germany, the chief dangers lie to the east, in the form of either endemic instability or the (increasingly remote) possibility of a resurgent Russia. For France,

---

38. Of course, credibility may be less important now that the Soviet Union is gone, but only if the members of the alliance are willing to accept a looser association in which prompt and unanimous responses are neither expected nor required.

39. See Duke, *New European Security Disorder*, pp. 297–98.

Italy, and Spain, spillover from civil strife in North Africa looms ever larger, mingled with vague fears of German political and economic ascendancy. Turkey and Greece continue to eye each other warily, while facing internal challenges of their own and casting worried glances at the Balkan cauldron. The United States is increasingly tugged toward Asia or preoccupied by conditions at home or in its immediate neighborhood. As the alliance seeks to formulate new missions, therefore, it is no longer obvious even where it ought to look.

The clearest sign of the eroding geostrategic consensus has been the protracted debate over NATO expansion. Once again the contrast with the cold war era is instructive. Bipolarity divided Europe neatly between east and west, with only a handful of minor anomalies.[40] Both sides knew who was in the other's camp, and each refrained from excessive interference in the other's sphere of influence. Now, however, it is no longer clear what the "Atlantic alliance" should encompass, and potential members are defined neither by shared threats or geographic interests, but by social, economic, political, and military criteria. Shorn of an external threat to focus the mind (and the debate), advocates and opponents of expansion invoke rival theories to support their positions and end up talking past each other.[41] Even the recent decision to invite Poland, Hungary, and the Czech Republic to begin negotiations for accession featured a last-minute conflict over the exclusion of Romania, a further sign of the absence of clear criteria identifying whom NATO is for and whom it is against.

These problems are not due to a failure of will, vision, or political skill on the part of NATO's present leaders. Rather, they are a direct consequence of the lack of clarity inherent in multipolarity. New policy initiatives cannot alter these structural problems; they can only respond to them.

---

40. Switzerland, Austria, and Sweden were pro-Western neutrals, while Yugoslavia and Romania occupied anomalous positions in the East.

41. In general, advocates of expansion invoke the basic logic of liberal institutionalism, arguing that incorporating eastern Europe within Western institutions (including NATO) will bolster their emerging democracies and dampen security competition among them. By contrast, opponents tend to rely on the logic of the balance of power, arguing that expanding NATO will alarm Russia, threaten the presently benign state of East-West relations, and involve the United States in areas where it has no immediate strategic interest. For examples of the competing views, see Clinton, *National Security Strategy*, p. 27; Talbott, "Why NATO Should Grow"; Brown, "Flawed Logic of NATO Expansion"; and Mandelbaum, "NATO Expansion."

AN EXPANDED RANGE OF OPTIONS. The problems just described are exacerbated by another central feature of multipolarity: each of the major actors now enjoys a wider range of options. This feature makes it more difficult to gain consensus within the alliance (because most members have more options to consider) and magnifies the problems of credibility and strategic definition already discussed.

Under bipolarity, the looming threat from the Warsaw Pact gave the alliance members relatively little latitude in dealing with each other or with other significant states. This is not to say that differences did not arise and were not pursued, of course. France's independent military policy was perhaps the most obvious example, but the West German policy of Ostpolitik also involved a partial departure from the alliance consensus. Yet the fear of losing U.S. protection and the importance of preserving NATO solidarity placed clear limits on each state's freedom of action.

The range of choice is much greater now. Evidence of this enhanced latitude includes Germany's decision to reunify in the face of British and French misgivings, its subsequent decision to recognize Croatia and Slovenia in the face of U.S. and European opposition, and its recent willingness to maintain cordial ties with revolutionary Iran despite clear U.S. opposition.[42] Other signs include the growing divergence in European and U.S. policies toward Iraq (and especially the European refusal to pressure Iraq into full compliance with the United Nations Special Commission (UNSCOM) inspections regime) as well as the tepid European reaction to the Indian and Pakistani nuclear tests in May 1998.

Moreover, now that the Europeans need not maintain a united front against Moscow (or against Washington, for that matter), informal coalitions within the alliance will be more significant. Coalitions within the alliance are hardly unprecedented (the Anglo-American special relationship comes immediately to mind), but such developments will be more common in the future. Individual states are likely to pursue cooperative partnerships with great powers outside of Europe (Japan, China, Russia), even in the absence of a transatlantic consensus.

A TRULY UNITED EUROPE? A final possibility is the continued coalescence of the European Union and its emergence as a more or less unified actor on the world stage. Interestingly, much of the recent momentum

42. See Charles Lane, "Germany's New Ostpolitik," *Foreign Affairs*, vol. 74, no. 6 (1995).

for institutional expansion in Europe has been driven by a desire to head off a return to the competitive power politics of the past. Thus French leaders sought to enmesh a reunified Germany in stronger European institutions, British leaders wanted to ensure that the United States remained fully committed as a counterweight to Germany and as a pacifying presence, and German chancellor Helmut Kohl sought to reassure his neighbors so as not to trigger defensive responses that might strengthen hard-line nationalists in Germany itself.[43]

Although the United States publicly endorsed European integration throughout the cold war, its actions both facilitated and inhibited this process. On the positive side, the U.S. presence reduced European fears of other European states, making it easier for former adversaries to cooperate. But the dominant U.S. role impeded the emergence of a separate European defense establishment and stifled the emergence of an independent European defense identity. With the passing of the cold war, however, calls for strengthening the European pillar have grown, and some tentative steps (such as the formation of the European Rapid Reaction Corps) have been taken. If the U.S. role continues to decline, and if the European powers can overcome lingering fears of each other, then the as-yet unrealized vision of a common European foreign policy might become a reality.[44]

Strengthening the European Union would have ambiguous implications for the United States. By reducing the likelihood of great-power war in Europe, unification would reduce the danger of a war that might engage the United States. Yet further integration would also make Europe a more potent political and economic rival. Even if relations remained relatively harmonious, the United States would quickly discover that a unified Europe was a formidable obstacle when its interests conflicted with ours. Some form of transatlantic partnership might survive, but it would be a vast departure from its past or present condition. Indeed, now that European unity is not needed to deter the Soviet Union,

43. See Art, "Why Europe Needs the United States and NATO."
44. Scholars with similar theoretical predilections still reach different conclusions about the prospects for European unity. For example, John Mearsheimer believes that the return to multipolarity will lead to intense security competition in western Europe, while Kenneth Waltz suggests that the end of bipolarity "may produce the final push to unification." See Mearsheimer, "Back to the Future"; and Waltz, "Emerging Structure of World Politics," p. 70.

the United States will be increasingly suspicious of European political integration and may even try to subvert it.[45]

In sum, the playing field of world politics has changed in fundamental ways. The increased range of choice means that the range of acceptable public debate has broadened: previously excluded possibilities are becoming serious options, thereby altering public discourse on foreign policy and in turn shaping how traditional allies see one another. Among other things, these developments mean that the history of the past forty-five years is an unreliable guide to the future, and one simply cannot take the transatlantic community for granted.

As the U.S. role decreases—as it almost certainly will—its influence will decline and the probability of transatlantic disputes will rise. As these disputes increase, the U.S. incentive to remain involved will decline even further, reducing even more its ability to lead. The clear possibility of this sort of downward spiral reflects the basic fact that there is no natural equilibrium for the transatlantic partnership now that the Soviet threat is gone. Enlightened statecraft may defy these pressures and preserve the status quo for a time, but diplomatic virtuosity and democratic enlightenment are weak reeds on which to rest the long-term future of the alliance.

The Globalization of World Markets

A second systemic feature affecting the transatlantic partnership is the simultaneous expansion and regionalization of world markets. Some of these developments reinforce existing incentives for transatlantic cooperation, but others are likely to undermine it.

What are the basic trends? First, as is well known, there has been a remarkable expansion of international trade and investment throughout the postwar period. The total volume of global trade grew by over 11 percent a year from 1950 to 1992, and for the countries of the Organization for Economic Cooperation and Development (OECD), the per-

---

45. NATO is in for serious strains whether Europe continues to unify or not. If European integration continues, then the need for the U.S. military presence will decline further, and European deference to U.S. wishes will evaporate. If European integration unravels, however, the United States is likely to try to distance itself from Europe's growing quarrels. Either way, the present partnership will be fundamentally altered.

centage of GDP arising from foreign trade doubled (from 21 percent to 43 percent) between 1970 and 1992. Even the United States, whose involvement in world trade remains comparatively modest, is more dependent on foreign markets than ever before.[46]

The expansion of global markets has been accompanied by a simultaneous trend toward regionalization. Intra-European trade has risen from 63 percent of total European trade in 1968 to more than 70 percent in the 1990s, while trade among the three North American Free Trade Agreement (NAFTA) countries (the United States, Mexico, and Canada) now composes roughly 40 percent of their total trade. Intra-Asian trade has grown from 37 percent of total Asian trade in 1968 to nearly 50 percent in the 1990s, although some countries (such as Japan) now trade more outside the region than within it.[47] This trend toward regionalization is also reflected by renewed progress toward European integration, beginning with the Single European Act in 1986 and proceeding through the Maastricht agreement in 1991 and the continued effort to create a single European currency. Although progress has been more difficult than many once hoped, the overall direction of the past decade has been sharply positive. A similar tendency may be observed on the other side of the Atlantic as well, most notably in the NAFTA.[48]

46. In 1996 U.S. exports plus imports equaled 23.6 percent of GNP. The statistics in this paragraph were taken from *Statistical Abstract of the United States* (Washington, D.C.: U.S. Government Printing Office, 1997); *Handbook of International Trade and Development Statistics 1994* (New York: United Nations Conference on Trade and Development, 1994), pp. 2, 28–29; *Statistical Yearbook 1994* (New York: United Nations, 1996); and *International Trade Statistics Yearbook, 1993* (New York: United Nations, 1995).

47. These figures are drawn from Kym Anderson and Hege Norheim, "History, Geography, and Regional Economic Integration," in Kym Anderson and Richard Blackhurst, eds., *Regional Integration and the Global Trading System* (New York: St. Martin's, 1993). According to a different source, intra-EEC exports increased from 50.1 percent of total EEC exports in 1969–71 to 58 percent in 1993. See *Handbook of International Trade and Development Statistics 1993*. The sources and impact of "regionalization" are complex and contested, but the most sophisticated recent analysis concludes that "intraregional concentrations of trade are growing" and further notes that "while many regional agreements have in the past been more show than substance, the new breed of free trade areas has real effects." See Jeffrey T. Frankel, *Regional Trading Blocs in the World Economic System* (Washington, D.C.: Institute for International Economics, 1997), pp. 112–13, 229; also see Miles Kahler, *Regional Futures and Transatlantic Economic Relations* (New York: Council on Foreign Relations Press, 1995).

48. See Andrew Hurrell, "Explaining the Resurgence of Regionalism in World Politics," *Review of International Studies*, vol. 21, no. 4 (1995).

At the same time, the focus of U.S. foreign economic activity is shifting from Europe to Asia. Asia surpassed Europe as the primary target of U.S. trade in 1983, and trade with Asia now composes roughly 34 percent of total U.S. trade, while trade with Europe composes 23 percent. The size of U.S. direct foreign investment in Europe is still roughly three times the level of U.S. investment in Asia, but the gap is closing as the Asian economies become more receptive to foreign investors.[49] In the meantime, several European states (especially Germany) have established substantial economic positions in central and eastern Europe, even though the levels of trade and investment remain modest compared with other regions and with the size of the investors' internal markets.[50]

These developments will affect transatlantic relations in at least three ways. First, the growing importance of world trade and the benefits of preserving a relatively open world economy give the industrialized powers a common interest in preventing either a destructive return to protectionism or a serious erosion in the international security environment. Economic interdependence may or may not foster peace, but peace does appear to be a powerful promoter of interdependence. Open economic orders thrive on stability because states worry less about relative gains when they do not fear their partners, and investors worry less about sending assets abroad when the danger of political upheavals is remote. The problem, however, is whether the present international order can survive the shift from bipolarity to multipolarity. Freed from its role as leader of the anti-Soviet alliance, the United States will be less willing to let its allies run long-term trade surpluses and less willing to pay the other costs of maintaining an open order. Thus, despite the general in-

49. In 1980 U.S. direct investment in Europe was roughly $96 billion, while investment in Asia was roughly $23 billion. By 1994 investment in Asia had grown to $108 billion, while investment in Europe was roughly $300 billion. These calculations are based on data found in *Direction of Trade Statistics Yearbook, 1996* (Washington, D.C.: International Monetary Fund, 1996), and *Statistical Abstract of the United States 1996* (Washington, D.C.: U.S. Department of Commerce, 1996).

50. For example, combined German investment in Czechoslovakia, Poland, Hungary, and Russia was approximately $58 million in 1989, but had grown to nearly $2.7 billion by 1994. Similarly, German trade with central Europe and Russia totaled approximately $20 billion in 1989, but grew to nearly $60 billion by 1995. See *International Direct Investment Statistics Yearbook, 1995* (Paris: OECD, 1996); and *Direction of Trade Statistics Yearbook, 1996*.

terest in an open economic order, the present system is likely to come under growing pressures in the future.[51]

Second, the gradual shift in the direction of U.S. economic involvement is likely to foster further transatlantic estrangement, particularly if European economic integration continues. Economic interests do not determine security commitments, of course, and both Europe and America will retain significant economic links for the foreseeable future. Over time, however, the growing economic importance of Asia is certain to receive greater attention from U.S. policymakers, just as the rise of China and the uncertain security situation in Asia are receiving greater attention from U.S. defense planners. The Asian financial crisis and the Indian and Pakistani nuclear tests are likely to reinforce these trends, and because time and resources are finite, they herald an inevitable decline in the level of attention devoted to Europe.[52] Although area specialists and bureau chiefs will continue to keep watch on their appointed regions, high-level officials will devote less time, less energy, and, most important, less political capital to areas whose relative importance is declining. European leaders will respond by paying less attention to Washington, thereby reinforcing the erosion in transatlantic cohesion.

Third, the rapid expansion of global markets and the growing popularity of market-oriented social policies could have important indirect effects on U.S.-European security relations. For all their benefits, unfettered free markets can also be powerful engines of political and social instability. Rapid globalization is likely to have profound and unpredictable effects on much of the world, including the advanced industrial countries. Outside the NATO region, these pressures are likely to generate political instability, mass migration, and even revolution, thereby creating security problems that could affect the alliance directly. Within the NATO countries, globalization will threaten specific sectors with rapid

51. Analyses supporting these arguments include Barry Buzan, "Economic Structure and International Security: The Limits of the Liberal Case," *International Organization*, vol. 38, no. 4 (1984); Robert Powell, "Absolute and Relative Gains in International Relations Theory," *American Political Science Review*, vol. 85, no. 4 (1991); and Gowa, *Allies, Adversaries and International Trade*.

52. The attention lavished on Asia during Clinton's first term made many Europeans nervous, fears that were reinforced by then-secretary of state Warren Christopher's warnings against an excessively "Eurocentric" perspective and his publicly stated belief in the future "primacy of Asia." Ironically, the Bosnian tragedy was probably a godsend for Europhiles, because it forced the Clinton administration to devote more attention to Europe than it initially intended. See Gordon, "Recasting the Atlantic Alliance," p. 39.

26   Stephen M. Walt

obsolescence, leading to rising levels of discontent and greater pressure for protectionist measures. One could even imagine, though it is an unlikely scenario, growing disenchantment with liberal democracy within the industrialized West should these economic pressures become severe.[53]

In short, although the world economy's expansion has been a notable achievement of the post–World War II period, its contemporary features do not bode well for the transatlantic partnership. At a minimum, they increase the strains that the alliance is likely to face, without adding a corresponding element of cohesion.

The Changing Security Agenda

The final dimension of systemic change concerns the specific nature of the security threats now facing the alliance. Whatever its other rationales may have been, NATO's main purpose was to defend Europe from a Soviet attack. In practice, this meant deterring either a large-scale conventional armored invasion or a Soviet nuclear strike (or both) and attempting to ensure that a conventional attack would fail.

The demise of the Warsaw Pact has removed these missions, and the danger of a rapid Russian resurgence seems increasingly remote. In its place, however, are more ambiguous, variegated, and interrelated dangers. Because the nature of contemporary European security threats is more difficult to define and measure, fashioning a collective response will be harder than developing a common response to the Soviet threat.[54] What are these new threats, and is the alliance still an appropriate means of addressing them?

POLITICAL INSTABILITY. The first concern—from which many others flow—is political instability. The collapse of the Warsaw Pact has left eastern Europe facing an uncertain future, as these societies attempt to fashion democratic political orders while making a simultaneous

53. See Bruce D. Porter, "Is the Zone of Peace Stable? Sources of Stress and Conflict in Industrial Democracies in Post–Cold War Europe," *Security Studies*, vol. 4, no. 3 (1995).

54. See James Goodby, "Can Collective Security Work? Reflections on the European Case," in Chester Crocker and Fen Osler Hampson, with Pamela Aall, eds., *Managing Global Chaos: Sources of and Responses to International Conflict* (Washington, D.C.: U.S. Institute of Peace Press, 1996).

transition to market-oriented economies. Farther east, Russia and the newly independent states face even more daunting efforts at institution building.

These events have reminded Europeans that instability can affect their own prosperity and sense of security. Nowhere is this more evident than in the dramatic rise in immigration (legal or otherwise) following the collapse of Communist rule. Roughly 3 million asylum seekers entered western Europe between 1989 and 1994, including nearly 1.5 million in Germany alone. Not only do such developments place further demands on the European welfare state, but rising immigrant populations may trigger nationalist backlashes that could undermine the prevailing atmosphere of European amity.[55] Political instability is also a potential source of terrorism, and western Europe has not been immune from these spillover effects either.[56]

Unfortunately, threats arising from political instability do not lend themselves to collective action by a transatlantic security organization. These threats will not affect each state equally, and it will be difficult to convince alliance members to do much when their own interests are not directly affected. The extended debate over whether to intervene in Bosnia illustrates the problem perfectly, as does the growing controversy over whether to keep NATO forces there.[57] NATO's members have acted unilaterally when their own interests were directly engaged (for example, Germany has provided a modest amount of economic aid to Russia and to several eastern European states, and the United States has actively promoted denuclearization in Russia, Ukraine, Belarus, and Kazakhstan), but collective responses have been conspicuously absent.

55. See *Trends in International Migration* (Paris: OECD/Continuous Reporting System on Migration, 1995), p. 195. For a useful discussion of the social and political effects of migration, see Ole Wæver and others, *Identity, Migration, and the New Security Regime in Europe* (New York: St. Martin's, 1993), especially chap. 8. For useful background, see Myron Weiner, "Security, Stability, and International Migration," *International Security*, vol. 17, no. 3 (1992/93).

56. Western Europe was the site of 760 terrorist incidents between 1989 and 1994, the second highest total for any region. Altogether 428 persons were killed or wounded in these attacks, which was a significantly lower number of casualties than in other regions. See *Patterns of Global Terrorism* (Washington, D.C.: U.S. Department of State, 1995).

57. As James Goodby notes, "the concept [of collective security]—especially the notion that military forces should be used to uphold rules of behavior—has been catastrophically damaged in its first major post–cold war test in Europe." "Can Collective Security Work?" p. 238.

OUT-OF-AREA PROBLEMS. Now that NATO no longer faces ninety-plus Soviet divisions, security threats outside Europe are receiving relatively greater attention. Such concerns are not entirely new, of course, as NATO has dealt with out-of-area problems throughout its history.[58] The 1991 Gulf War demonstrates that the alliance can be an especially effective mechanism for coordinating a military response to events outside NATO's formal boundaries, and recent NATO summits have devoted greater attention to out-of-area missions.

Although these initiatives may enhance NATO's ability to respond to regional crises and limited out-of-area contingencies, they are unlikely to provide an enduring basis for transatlantic cooperation. Events outside the NATO area will rarely affect all members to the same extent, and the costs of meeting these challenges are going to increase as each state's military capabilities decline. Even if all members agreed on the need to respond, the temptation to free ride would be considerable. Most important, NATO's members remain reluctant to commit themselves to such activities in advance. Thus, although the 1992 Brussels summit recognized "that certain events outside the Treaty area may affect . . . common interests," it called only for "consultations on such events . . . based on recognition of those common interests" and noted that "those Allies in a position to do so may respond to requests by sovereign nations whose security and independence are threatened."[59] In other words, NATO members are free to consult with each other and to take action outside the NATO region (something they were already free to do anyway), but there is no obligation to do anything. If that is as far as the alliance is willing to go, then out-of-area missions will not provide the glue to hold NATO together.

WEAPONS OF MASS DESTRUCTION. Renewed attention has also focused on the proliferation of weapons of mass destruction (or WMD, to include nuclear, biological, or chemical weapons). The spread of WMD and ballistic missile technology was identified as a special problem at

---

58. For background, see Douglas T. Stuart and William T. Tow, *The Limits of Alliance: NATO Out-of-Area Problems since 1949* (Johns Hopkins University Press, 1990); for a more theoretical treatment, see Charles A. Kupchan, "NATO and the Persian Gulf: Examining Intra-Alliance Behavior," *International Organization*, vol. 42, no. 2 (1988).

59. Final Communiqué of the North Atlantic Council Ministerial Session in Brussels, 9–10 December 1992; quoted in Duke, *New European Security Disorder*, p. 298.

the 1991 NATO summit in Rome, catalyzed in part by the danger of "loose nukes" in the former Soviet Union, the nuclear ambitions of countries such as North Korea and Iraq, and the continued spread of relevant nuclear technology. In 1994 the North Atlantic Council endorsed existing efforts to control such weaponry and committed the member states to begin a series of political and military initiatives intended to "prevent proliferation from occurring or . . . to reverse it by diplomatic means."[60]

The otherwise laudable effort to arrest the spread of WMD will not be enough to sustain a coherent and cohesive security commitment among NATO's present members. First, there is little evidence to suggest that the alliance is willing to go beyond rhetorical condemnation (for instance, by using its economic or military power to punish or disarm potential proliferators). European willingness to confront Iraq has declined steadily since the 1991 Gulf War, and the European states are unlikely to impose significant sanctions on India or Pakistan in the wake of their recent nuclear tests.[61] Second, there is a direct connection between the overall health of the alliance and its shared interest in preventing proliferation. If NATO's members begin to doubt that the alliance can meet their security requirements, the desire to hedge their bets by acquiring WMD is likely to increase. In particular, Germany's current opposition to acquiring a nuclear arsenal would almost certainly decline if it concluded that allied support was no longer reliable.[62]

Thus the ability of the alliance members to act together against the threat of WMD proliferation itself depends on whether the alliance can sustain a broad multilateral commitment to the members' security. The threat from WMD will be one item on NATO's agenda, but it is not a sufficient condition for its continued existence.

THE PERILS OF RENATIONALIZATION. A final—and in some ways, the most important—item on the new security agenda is the danger of renewed rivalry within Europe itself. This danger is not really new, of course, insofar as the memory of the fratricidal bloodlettings of the first half of

60. See North Atlantic Council, "Alliance Policy Framework on Proliferation of Weapons of Mass Destruction, June 9, 1994," NATO Review, vol. 42, no. 3 (1994), pp. 28–29.

61. The United States is legally obligated to impose sanctions, but it remains to be seen how extensively they will be enforced.

62. Similar cautions apply in the case of Japan. I am not suggesting that either state is likely to acquire WMD; only that their willingness to do so will be heavily influenced by their confidence in their alliance partners.

this century provided both the initial impetus for European integration and the unprecedented U.S. commitment to Europe's defense. As long as the Soviet threat overshadowed Europe and gave the United States a reason to remain, however, these fears were muted and almost forgotten.

The passing of the cold war has brought this benevolent condition to an end. The question is: will the European states continue to pursue a collective approach to self-defense, either in the context of a European entity or in partnership with the United States, or will the main European powers gradually revert to independent action? As Robert Art has shown, the desire to ward off a renationalization of European security politics played an important role in the European effort to refashion the institutional arrangements for European security affairs after 1989. The success of these efforts casts at least some doubt on the claim that the end of the cold war inevitably presages a swift return to balance-of-power politics. Instead, awareness of the risks of renationalization has led the principal European powers to try to head off these possibilities before they occur. Instead of merely balancing German power, for example, Britain and France have sought to enmesh Germany within a larger European framework. Instead of simply reasserting German autonomy, Chancellor Helmut Kohl has sought to reassure Germany's neighbors so as not to provoke either a balancing response by others or a nationalist resurgence at home. And all three states have sought to preserve an active U.S. role, seeing it as the most obvious and effective means of warding off renewed security competition within Europe.[63]

Here is where the transatlantic partnership can play an especially valuable role. A visible U.S. role in Europe effectively insulates the European powers from each other and reduces their need to amass power to meet other external challenges. Thus, as Charles Glaser suggests, the fundamental purpose of the alliance—preserving peace in Europe—has not changed. The Russian threat may be gone, but the danger of renewed great-power competition is real, and NATO remains the best way to deal with it.[64]

63. See Art, "Why Europe Needs the United States and NATO." In the same vein, Barry Buzan argues that "What is to be feared is not military conflicts in Western Europe, but that a security-driven relationship would mean a process of disintegration, of unraveling of the EC." See his "Introduction: The Changing Security Agenda in Europe," in Wæver and others, *Identity, Migration, and the New Security Agenda*, pp. 9–10.

64. See Glaser, "Why NATO Is Still Best."

The central question, however, is whether this role can be sustained through public support in the United States. Advocates of a continued U.S. role face something of a paradox, for, if relations in Europe remain tranquil, the need for the U.S. "pacifier" will be hard to demonstrate. But if relations in Europe deteriorate, then the costs and risks of involvement will rise even though U.S. security is not directly affected (assuming no new hegemon has arisen). Despite the confident rhetoric of transatlantic harmony and the current commitment to expansion, therefore, the long-term future of the alliance is still uncertain.

The discussion thus far has focused on changes occurring at the systemic level: in relations between states and in the specific security threats that they face. Foreign policy is also shaped by developments occurring within each state, however, and the impact of domestic factors is probably greater now than it was during the height of the cold war. Bipolarity imposed fairly tight constraints on the great powers (the United States and the Soviet Union were inevitable rivals and worked hard to keep their allies in line), but the current structure of world politics places fewer constraints on state action. As systemic pressures ease, unit-level forces come more powerfully into play. Accordingly, the next step is to consider how domestic developments in Europe and the United States are likely to affect the security relationship between them.

The Domestic Sphere

The sweeping changes that have occurred in the structure of world politics have been accompanied by major changes within the member states of the alliance.[65] Since 1989, we have witnessed the reunification of Germany, a renaissance of secessionism in Quebec, antigovernment strikes and the fall of the conservative government in France and the United Kingdom, a political transformation in Italy, a Republican resurgence in the U.S. Congress, and the end of socialist rule in Spain. Democracy and capitalism have spread to eastern Europe and the former Soviet bloc (albeit unevenly and imperfectly), while the hegemony of

65. Indeed, the end of bipolarity was largely the result of domestic developments within the Soviet Union, and even unabashed structuralists such as Kenneth Waltz acknowledge that "structural change begins in a system's unit, and then unit-level and structural causes interact." See his "Emerging Structure," p. 49.

the Liberal Democratic party in Japan has been partly broken and a degree of domestic political reform has begun. These developments are probably not coincidental; rather, they are in part a product of the cold war's end and an important factor shaping how each state is responding to that event. Rather than examining specific policies, however, I focus on three aspects of domestic politics that are likely to present long-term challenges to the alliance itself.

The Erosion of State Power

Throughout modern history, external rivalries between states have been an important instrument in forging both cohesive societies and powerful state structures. In Charles Tilly's well-known phrase, "War made the state and the state made war."[66] This trend continued during the twentieth century and into the cold war: truly modern central planning first emerged in the First World War; the Stalinist state was created to deal with an anticipated war with the West; and the creation of a strong federal government in the United States was driven primarily by national security concerns as well. Foreign challenges justified more extensive social welfare programs, lavish government support for scientific research, and the nurturing of autonomous national security establishments (even in societies with powerful antimilitary biases) and probably contributed to national cohesion in less visible and immediate ways as well.[67]

The end of the cold war has reversed this process, at least temporarily. In the absence of an imminent external threat, it has become more difficult to justify large and intrusive government establishments and harder to persuade citizens to pay the taxes needed to support a powerful central authority. Even where the willingness is still there, it may not be possible to sustain the same levels of social support. The absence of an external enemy facilitates efforts to devolve state power from the center to lower levels (for example, to the separate states in the United States)

66. See Charles Tilly, *The Formation of National States in Western Europe* (Princeton University Press, 1975), 42; Charles Tilly, *Coercion, Capital, and European States, A.D. 990–1990* (Oxford: Blackwell, 1990).

67. On these developments, see Bruce D. Porter, *War and the Rise of the State* (New York: Basic Books, 1994); and Bartholomew H. Sparrow, *From the Outside In: World War II and the American State* (Princeton University Press, 1996).

and has encouraged the emergence of separatist movements in a number of countries. Put differently, national unity flourishes in the face of a distinct external challenge, while disunity is more likely when an external "other" is less visible.[68] These trends are also reflected in (and reinforced by) the gradual abandonment of conscription in the industrialized world, which has weakened a traditional mechanism for fostering patriotism and national unity.[69] Although nationalism is alive and well and the state is still the dominant political form, public support for ambitious governmental programs (including ambitious defense and foreign policy initiatives) is declining.

Other developments are reinforcing these trends. In Europe, economic stagnation and growing fiscal strains threaten the viability of the existing welfare state and will force European societies to make very difficult choices in the years ahead. These problems could be compounded if multipolarity and globalization trigger new demands for protectionism, if a global recession leads to even higher levels of unemployment, and if immigrant populations are blamed for future economic woes. The individualistic ethos of contemporary capitalism could accelerate this trend by encouraging citizens to act solely in their narrow self-interest. As citizens become more individualistic, the collectivity will find it more difficult to make legitimate claims on their time, wealth, or lives, particularly when there is no clear-cut external threat to justify a strong central state.

For these reasons, among others, state power is declining on both sides of the Atlantic. By itself, this trend does not threaten the transatlantic partnership directly. Yet to the extent that the alliance rests on a shared set of interests or goals and on the ability of national governments to make credible commitments to mutual defense (and conceivably to other broader security goals), any erosion in central state capacities presents an indirect threat to NATO's effectiveness. As governments are less able to extract resources through taxation and as demands from fractious and

---

68. See Michael C. Desch, "War and Strong States, Peace and Weak States?" *International Organization*, vol. 50, no. 2 (1996); and Susan Strange, *The Retreat of the State: The Diffusion of Power in the World Economy* (Cambridge University Press, 1996). For important contrasting assessments, see Ethan D. Kapstein, *Governing the Global Economy: International Finance and the State* (Harvard University Press, 1994); and "Survey of the World Economy: The Future of the State," The *Economist*, September 20, 1977.

69. See "Conscription: It's Had Its Day," The *Economist*, February 10, 1996, 48–49; and Barry R. Posen, "Nationalism, the Mass Army, and Military Power," *International Security*, vol. 18, no. 3 (1993).

self-serving interest groups increase, the ability of democratic leaders to make reliable commitments to their foreign partners may decline. Indeed, when states cannot even define a "national interest," it becomes harder for allies to be sure that they have interests in common.

Demographic Shifts and Generational Change

A second domestic trend is generational and demographic change, especially in the United States. As symbolized by the past two U.S. presidential elections, in which decorated World War II veterans (George Bush and Bob Dole) were defeated by men born *after* World War II, one of whom had avoided military service, the 1990s are witnessing the gradual departure of the generation for whom the Depression, World War II, and the early cold war were defining historical events. The familiar litanies of transatlantic partnership will not resonate as loudly for the cohort that is now moving into key ministries, legislative seats, and eventually into presidential mansions.[70] And the cold war partnership between Europe and America will have even less meaning for those now in high school or college or for those children for whom the cold war itself will be a distant (and largely irrelevant) historical episode. These new elites may recognize the value of transatlantic cooperation and endeavor to preserve it, but that cooperation will not generate the reflexive emotional salience that it did for their parents and grandparents.

Demographic trends within the United States will reinforce a diminished focus on Europe. America's geopolitical focus has been directed toward Europe for most of its history, in part because the great powers were all European and their actions bore close watching even from an ocean away.[71] The cultural and ethnic connection between Europe and America was also important, as most Americans traced their own ancestry to Europe and saw European civilization as the wellspring of American political culture as well. The concentration of U.S. population along the eastern seaboard reinforced this tendency, while the western United States remained less populous, less prosperous, and less influential.

---

70. This tendency is readily apparent in the 1994 class of Republican U.S. congressmen, whose obvious nationalist convictions were accompanied by considerable skepticism about the value of multilateral solutions to U.S. security problems.

71. A concise summary of the evolving relationship is Miles Kahler and Werner Link, *Europe and America: A Return to History* (New York: Council on Foreign Relations Press, 1996).

Conditions today are quite different. The past four decades have witnessed a profound westward shift in the U.S. population, and this trend is continuing.[72] In addition, the non-European population of the United States is increasing steadily and is concentrated in regions lying outside the Cambridge-Washington corridor.[73] Moreover, the main waves of European immigration occurred several generations ago, and assimilation and intermarriage have diluted the sense of identification or affinity with the Old Country.[74] More recent immigrants from Asia or Latin America are more likely to retain these cultural affinities and more likely to hold strong views about U.S. policy toward these areas. Like the economic trends discussed in the previous section, these macro-forces will make it difficult to sustain the same level of elite consensus that characterized U.S. foreign policy during the heyday of the Atlantic alliance. Instead of being guided by an elite group of East Coast internationalists, committed to Europe by family backgrounds, personal experiences, and professional affiliations, U.S. foreign policy will be shaped by a more diverse group of elites whose ethnic characteristics, geographic points of reference, and professional experiences will not grant Europe pride of place. Their ascendance does not sound a death knell for the alliance, but preserving it will certainly be more difficult.

Public Opinion, Beliefs, and Attitudes

A final element of contemporary domestic politics concerns the nature of domestic ideologies, belief systems, and public attitudes. Specifically, how will fundamental political attitudes shape relations within

72. In 1950 approximately 27 percent of the U.S. population lived in the Northeast, while the West contained a mere 13.7 percent. In 1995, by contrast, the West had grown to 21.9 percent of the U.S. population, while the Northeast had fallen to 19.6 percent. The U.S. Bureau of the Census also predicts that the fastest growing states in the period 1993–2020 will be Nevada, Hawaii, California, and Washington; California (already the most populous state in the country) is expected to add another 16 million persons by 2020. See *Statistical Abstract of the United States, 1996*; and *Population Profile of the United States 1995*, Current Population Reports, Special Studies Series P23-189 (Washington, D.C.: U.S. Department of Commerce, 1995).

73. The percentage of U.S. citizens of European origin will decline from 80 percent in 1980 to 64 percent in 2020, while the percentages of Hispanics will rise from 6 percent to 15 percent and the percentage of Asians will rise from 2 percent to 7 percent. See *Statistical Abstract of the United States: 1994* (Washington, D.C.: U.S. Bureau of the Census, 1994), p. 18.

74. It is also worth noting that these ancestral ties to Europe did not lead the United States to make a permanent military commitment to Europe until after World War II.

the alliance? How do citizens on both sides of the Atlantic regard each other, the present international environment, and the role of military force? Public attitudes can be a notoriously poor guide to the future, but they still pose a constraint on democratic leaders and illustrate the implications of many of the trends already discussed.

With respect to prevailing public norms, perhaps the most obvious change from the cold war era is the absence of ideological conflict among the great powers. With the partial exception of China, virtually all the great powers now embrace some form of democratic capitalism. Ideological conformity is strongest among the advanced industrial democracies in Europe and North America, which share similar domestic political and economic orders and have a shared cultural heritage as well. Although movement toward democracy has slowed since the heady days of 1989, the contrast with the cold war is still striking.[75]

Not surprisingly, many experts regard the absence of ideological conflict as a boon to the alliance, based on the by-now familiar argument that democracies are prone to cooperate and extremely reluctant to fight each other.[76] Scholars also suggest that modern industrial societies now see war as brutal, immoral, or silly (rather than as honorable, heroic, manly, or useful) and that this change in mass attitudes presents a profound barrier to war between these states.[77] Drawing on these and other arguments, Robert Jervis concludes that "the forces for peace among the developed countries are so overwhelming that impulses which under other circumstances would be destabilizing will not lead to violence."[78] If so, then relations between Europe and America should remain friendly even in the absence of a looming external threat, thereby facilitating continuation of the alliance.

75. See Samuel P. Huntington, *The Third Wave: Democratization in the Late Twentieth Century* (University of Oklahoma Press, 1996).

76. Useful guides to this debate include Steven E. Miller, Michael Brown, and Sean Lynn-Jones, eds., *Debating the Democratic Peace* (MIT Press, 1996); and Miriam Elman, ed., *Paths to Peace: Is Democracy the Answer?* (MIT Press, 1997).

77. See John Mueller, *Retreat from Doomsday: The Obsolescence of Major War* (New York: Basic Books, 1989).

78. Jervis believes that these changes are "irreversible" and argues that "the ties of mutual interest and identification, the altered psychology . . . the new supranational institutions, and the general sense that there is no reason for the developed countries to fight each other will remain." See his "Future of World Politics," pp. 53–55; and also Van Evera, "Primed for Peace."

Alas, this argument may be too optimistic, even if gloomier forecasts of democracy's future turn out to be mistaken.[79] First, if the absence of ideological conflict has eliminated a potential source of division within the alliance, it has also removed an important source of unity. The ideological nature of the Soviet challenge reinforced the value of transatlantic cooperation, giving the United States a powerful stake in its partners' economic and social health. Now that this danger is gone, however, there is neither a military nor a political rival to balance against.

Second, the absence of an ideological alternative to capitalism is likely to place the differences among the advanced industrial states in sharper relief and to permit invidious comparisons to arise. There are important historical differences between European and American notions of democratic rule, and these differences have taken on greater significance whenever political conflicts arose. The compatibility of domestic orders may be mostly in the eye of the beholder (a point that some liberal theorists now concede), and the present level of perceived ideological conformity could erode rapidly if political conflicts became more frequent or more intense.[80] And to the extent that democratic leaders are more responsive to their constituents than other leaders are, their ability to head off clashes of interest arising from internal pressures (for instance, over economic issues) will be limited.

In short, ideological conformity is neither a necessary nor a sufficient condition for either preserving the alliance or maintaining transatlantic cooperation. It may help keep the temperature of world politics from rising to dangerous levels, but it cannot prevent the inevitable clash of state interests. More important, ideological affinities will not overcome the reluctance to pay large costs or run large risks for the sake of other societies, unless doing so is seen as necessary to safeguard tangible (and selfish) national interests.

79. See Porter, "Is the Zone of Peace Stable?"
80. According to Ido Oren, U.S. leaders saw Wilhelmine Germany as less and less democratic as relations between the two states deteriorated before World War I, even though Germany was in fact becoming increasingly "liberal" and democratic during this period. Similarly, John Owen argues that pacific relations between more-or-less democratic states rest primarily on each side's *beliefs* that the other side is a liberal regime, independent of what the reality might be. See Ido Oren, "The Subjectivity of the 'Democratic Peace': Changing U.S. Perceptions of Imperial Germany," and John Owen, "How Liberalism Produces Democratic Peace," both in Miller, Brown, and Lynn-Jones, *Debating the Democratic Peace*.

Last but not least, how do European and American citizens think about the alliance, and what do their attitudes reveal about the future? The good news is that Allied populations continue to express a high regard for one another, and there is little evidence of serious political or security conflicts at the present time. According to a 1994 survey by the Chicago Council on Foreign Relations, for example, more than two-thirds of U.S. citizens regard European states such as Britain or Germany as "vital interests" (the percentage is even higher among elites), and they still regard Europe as more important than Asia by a margin of 49 percent to 21 percent. Americans believe that states such as Canada, Germany, France, and Great Britain are "friendly," and European populations generally reciprocate these attitudes.[81] At the most basic level, therefore, a solid sense of friendship continues to characterize U.S.-European relations.

The bad news, however, is the clear evidence of a declining U.S. commitment to internationalism in general and to Europe in particular. Although 65 percent of U.S. citizens still believe the United States should take "an active part" in world affairs (at least when the alternative is "staying out"), their support wanes when they are asked to consider potentially costly commitments. Foreign policy issues are increasingly regarded as among the least important problems facing the nation, and there is clear support for reducing intelligence gathering, defense spending, and economic and military aid to other countries. And although 56 percent of those surveyed in 1994 supported keeping the U.S. commitment to NATO "about the same," 37 percent favored cutbacks or a complete withdrawal and only 7 percent supported expansion. A majority of U.S. citizens supported the use of force in only two scenarios—a Russian invasion of Western Europe (54 percent) or an Iraqi invasion of Saudi Arabia (52 percent)—although elite support was higher in both scenarios. Eighty-three percent of Americans regard protecting the jobs of American workers as a "very important" goal, while only 24 percent believe that "protecting weaker nations from aggression" is equally important. Likewise, the percentage viewing "protecting allies" as "very important" has dropped from 61 percent in 1990 to 41 percent in 1994. And when people were asked to name the two or three biggest foreign policy

81. In a 1994 Louis Harris poll, the percentage of U.S. respondents describing a particular state as either a "close ally" or "friendly" were as follows: Canada, 96 percent; Great Britain, 88 percent; France, 80 percent; and Germany, 76 percent. See Survey Research Consultants International, *Index to International Public Opinion, 1993–94* (Westport: Greenwood Press, 1995), pp. 216–18.

problems facing the United States, their most frequent responses were "getting involved in affairs of other countries" (19 percent), "too much foreign aid to other countries" (16 percent), and "immigration" (12 percent). Six percent also mentioned "too much military involvement," the same total that mentioned the need for "a stronger foreign policy."[82]

Perhaps the most striking evidence is the unwillingness of most Americans to risk much blood or treasure for issues of little direct interest to the United States. In October 1995, for example, the Gallup Poll reported that 69 percent of the respondents supported the U.S. deployment to Bosnia (with 29 percent opposed), *assuming* that no U.S. lives would be lost. When asked to assume that the mission would lead to twenty-five U.S. deaths, however, only 31 percent supported deployment, and 64 percent of the respondents were against it.[83] A similar reluctance to bear any burden also explains why the Clinton administration kept lowering the estimated cost of NATO expansion as ratification approached. Americans may favor expanding NATO, but not if it is going to cost them very much.

Overall, these results reveal a considerable erosion in the internationalist consensus that has dominated U.S. opinion since the early 1950s.[84] Isolationist sentiments were never entirely absent, of course, but they were largely marginalized during the cold war. The collapse of the Soviet Union brought that era to an end, however, and the 1994 elections brought a group of vocal nativists to Congress, elevated individuals like Senator Jesse Helms to new positions of prominence, and triggered the retirement of prominent internationalists like Sam Nunn and Bill Bradley. The House proceeded to pass the ill-named "National Security Revitalization Act," which would have cut U.S. support for the United Nations and placed constraints on U.S. participation in peacekeeping missions, and Senate majority leader Robert Dole sponsored a bill forbidding U.S. troops to serve under foreign commanders.[85] Fear of public

82. See John E. Reilly, ed., *American Public Opinion and U.S. Foreign Policy, 1995* (Chicago Council on Foreign Relations, 1995).

83. The Gallup Poll, October 1995, reported in *Index of International Public Opinion, 1995–96*, p. 276.

84. Although Bob Dole eventually captured the Republican presidential nomination, Patrick Buchanan's surprising success in the Republican primary season suggests that his nativist message enjoys considerable grass roots support.

85. As Dole put it: "The American people will not tolerate American casualties for irresponsible internationalism." See Arthur Schlesinger Jr., "Back to the Womb? Isolationism's Renewed Threat," *Foreign Affairs*, vol. 74, no. 4 (1995).

opposition shaped the Clinton administration's response to the civil war in Bosnia, and the administration's belated decision to intervene brought unusually vocal skepticism within Congress. Thus pressure for a reduced international role is already strong and shows no signs of diminishing.

To be sure, there is still broad support for preserving American military superiority (provided it does not cost too much), and U.S. elites remain strongly committed to an active international role.[86] But such beliefs are not likely to survive the generational changes noted earlier and the fiscal constraints that loom ahead. Although the U.S. presence in Europe and Asia is not particularly expensive (especially given the host-nation support provided by our allies), pressure to bolster local economies by basing U.S. forces at home will grow as defense spending declines. And though downward pressure on the defense budget has subsided in recent years (after a sharp drop in 1990–92), this may be due more to President Clinton's awkward relationship with the U.S. military than to a strong public mandate for defense expenditures that are roughly 50 percent higher (as a percentage of GNP) than the NATO average. Barring a major change in the international environment, however, a further decline in U.S. capabilities and a concomitant reluctance to engage in costly international activities can be anticipated.

To sum up: public attitudes toward the alliance are neither especially alarming nor especially encouraging. Citizens in Europe and North America generally regard each other favorably and exhibit few signs of deeply rooted suspicion or hostility. There are growing doubts about the relationship, however; European populations are more likely to question U.S. leadership than they were a few years ago, and confidence in the credibility of present commitments appears to be waning as well.[87]

86. This is nowhere more apparent than in the Clinton administration itself, which has adopted lofty international goals despite waning U.S. resources. For a trenchant critique of Clinton's policies, see Michael Mandelbaum, "Foreign Policy as Social Work," *Foreign Affairs*, vol. 75, no. 1 (1996). Similarly, House speaker Newt Gingrich's characterization of himself as a "cheap hawk" suggests that he favors a powerful America but does not want to spend a lot to maintain it.

87. In 1995, 46 percent of Britons believed that the U.S. could be trusted "a great deal," down from 62 percent in 1981. In August 1991, 22 percent of Britons declared that their confidence in America to deal with world problems had "gone up," while 13 percent said it had "gone down." Two years later, only 8 percent reported that their confidence in the United States had increased, and 35 percent said it had declined. British approval of U.S. policy declined from 62 percent in February 1991 to 35 percent in September 1993, while the percent expressing disapproval of U.S. policy increased from 26 percent to 45 percent. Interestingly, 10 percent of Britons felt the United States should have the "leading role" in

The real danger is that these trends will be self-reinforcing over the longer term. As discussed above, declining confidence in U.S. leadership will encourage Europeans to act independently, further reducing U.S. willingness to remain involved, thereby forcing Europe to be more autonomous and leading to ever greater rancor and disillusionment. And the worst case would be not merely the dissolution of the alliance, but an end to the entire notion of an Atlantic community.

Conclusion

Wartime alliances rarely survive the defeat of the enemy. Given this expectation, NATO is already something of an anomaly. Its members remain committed to mutual defense even though the threat that brought them together has vanished, and they continue to sustain high levels of policy coordination and joint military planning. Moreover, NATO has responded to the end of the cold war by focusing on a number of new missions (such as regional stabilization, peacekeeping, the promotion of democracy, or the defense of human rights) and has revised its doctrine and decisionmaking procedures to reflect these new aims. Paradoxically, the fear that NATO might actually collapse has led a number of European states to reemphasize their desire for a continued U.S. presence. Thus NATO continues to exist for the obvious reason that its members still find it a useful way to handle a number of current security problems.[88]

But the security problems facing Europe today, in sharp contrast to the cold war, are much less important to the United States. As a result, they are unlikely to provide a reliable basis for extensive transatlantic cooperation. More important, virtually all of the trends discussed in this chapter point in the direction of diminished alliance cohesion, which means that the transatlantic partnership is facing an unprecedented challenge. What can be done to minimize the inevitable tensions and avoid a bitter divorce?

---

dealing with contemporary regional conflicts, but more than 30 percent believed that the United Nations should have that role. See *Index to International Public Opinion, 1993* (Westport, Conn.: Greenwood Press, 1994), pp. 212–13; and *Index to International Public Opinion, 1995–96* (Westport, Conn.: Greenwood Press, 1996), pp. 197–98.

88. On this point, see McCalla, "Persistence of NATO," and Wallander and Keohane, "Why Does NATO Persist?"

The first step is to accept the reality of diverging interests. Although policy differences can be submerged when circumstances require, they inevitably resurface when the need for unity is gone. We should therefore expect, and prepare ourselves for, a higher level of disagreement between Europe and America. Instead of striving for a common front on each and every issue, Europe and America will be better off encouraging each other to be more independent. Presumptions of unity will disappoint Europeans and Americans alike and create a higher risk of a disruptive backlash when serious disputes do arise. A looser partnership might also alleviate concerns about credibility, for if the United States and Europe learn not to expect unanimity, they will be less likely to view the inevitable disagreements as signs of a fading commitment.[89]

Instead of trying to give NATO an array of new tasks—thereby placing more burdens on an overloaded structure—the alliance should focus instead on goals that are relatively easy to meet and sustain. The minimum goal should be the preservation of a token U.S. presence in Europe and the maintenance of strong consultative mechanisms between Europe and the United States. The U.S. presence remains the best guarantee against a renewed security competition within Europe, while the existing consultative mechanisms reinforce each member's sense of membership in a larger political community and provide a means for coordinating policy when unexpected contingencies like the Falklands war or the invasion of Kuwait occur. The objective is to ensure that Europe and America continue to regard each other as reliable partners when common problems arise and to ensure that mechanisms for common action are in place when they are needed.[90]

---

89. In this regard, I share Charles Kupchan's belief, articulated in chapter 4, that the excessive ambition of the current policies will undermine the transatlantic community, as member states attempt to escape unwanted responsibilities. Yet Kupchan's own proposal for a new "Atlantic union" (based primarily on an expanded free trade zone) seems fanciful at best. A free trade zone would have modest economic effects, but would be politically contentious on both sides of the Atlantic. Moreover, I fail to see how subsuming several existing relationships (NATO, the WEU, and the EU) under a new label will solve any of the problems they currently face. Kupchan also suggests that an Atlantic union could absorb the central European states without appearing anti-Russian, but Moscow is unlikely to be fooled by such a transparent act of repackaging.

90. As Philip Gordon notes, "Perhaps the most important role alliance leaders can play today is to ensure that the institutions, patterns of communication, command structures and shared military capacities built up over the last 40 years are preserved. . . . So long as it is plausible that European and U.S. forces might be called upon to undertake military

Third, this approach implies that Europe should enjoy greater autonomy within the alliance—at the cost of diminished U.S. influence. Such an outcome is probably inevitable, and efforts to resist it will only provoke European resentment. U.S. leaders have recently become more receptive to independent European defense initiatives, and this policy should be continued as long as it does not threaten the U.S. role directly. By allowing existing forces to be "double-hatted" within NATO and the Western European Union (WEU), the new combined joint task force concept is a promising step despite the ambiguities that remain. By allowing NATO members to take action even when complete consensus or participation is lacking, this initiative may allow the alliance to address the security problems identified above while minimizing disruptive internal disputes.

Fourth, this perspective also suggests that the decision to expand NATO eastward was a strategic misstep. In addition to the obvious risk that it will jeopardize NATO's improved relations with Russia (a risk that is easy to overlook in light of Moscow's present weakness), the inclusion of Poland, Hungary, and the Czech Republic will place new burdens on an alliance whose shared interests are steadily eroding. Although the United States does have a stake in a stable and secure Europe, that interest is far less compelling than its earlier fear of a potential continental hegemon (such as Nazi Germany or the Soviet Union). As we have seen, a number of international and domestic developments are steadily eroding the bonds uniting Europe and America. It seems foolhardy, therefore, to be asking more of the alliance at a time when many of the forces that have held it together in the past are growing weaker.

The case for expansion rests on the belief that extending NATO membership eastward will eliminate the possibility of serious conflict in these regions, thereby keeping the costs and risks of expansion at a minimum.[91] Indeed, the Clinton administration's repeated claims that expansion will be neither costly nor risky reveals its own awareness that public support for the policy remains fragile. And if the

---

tasks together . . . it makes sense to preserve an integrated command structure and shared assets." See his "Recasting the Atlantic Alliance," p. 49.

91. The case for expansion contains a subtle contradiction. Advocates favor expansion because they believe that the spread of democratic institutions will eliminate the danger of conflict in Europe. But if this is true, then why are U.S. troops and security guarantees needed at all?

administation's optimistic forecasts are mistaken, the United States will end up paying most of the costs of expansion and will find itself embroiled in regional disputes in which it has few (if any) tangible interests. Thus the decision to expand NATO could easily jeopardize public support for any transatlantic military commitment and hasten a complete U.S. withdrawal.

Having taken that step, however, NATO's supporters will have to pay more attention to sustaining public support for a transatlantic military partnership. Structural forces and domestic pressures make the case more difficult to sell than it was during the height of the cold war, but there is still a prudential logic behind it. Transatlantic cooperation helped bring a generation of peace to a continent that had not known it for centuries, and NATO was a useful instrument for managing the potentially dangerous interregnum that followed the collapse of the Soviet Union. Thus, maintaining a modest U.S. military presence will buy time for Europe to adjust to the extraordinary changes that have occurred in the past ten years.

But nothing is permanent in international affairs, and NATO's past achievement must not blind us to its growing fragility. Instead of mindlessly extending guarantees to every potential trouble spot, and instead of basing our foreign policy on the presumption of permanent partnership, Europe and America should start preparing for a parting of the ways. It is going to happen anyway, and wise statecraft anticipates and exploits the tides of history, rather than engaging in a fruitless struggle against them.

Chapter 3

Integration as Security
Constructing a Europe at Peace

Ole Wæver

Nay, it is far more probable that in America, as in Europe, neighboring nations, acting under the impulse of opposite interests and unfriendly passions, would frequently be found taking different sides. Considering our distance from Europe, it would be more natural for these confederacies to apprehend danger from one another than from distant nations, and therefore that each of them should be more desirous to guard against the others by the aid of foreign alliances, than to guard against foreign dangers by alliances between themselves.

Federalist Paper No. 5

So far is the general sense of mankind from corresponding with the tenets of those who endeavor to lull asleep our apprehensions of discord and hostility between the States, in the event of disunion, that it has from long observation of the progress of society become a sort of axiom in politics, that vicinity or nearness of situation, constitutes nations natural enemies.

Federalist Paper No. 6
The Federalist, on the New Constitution,
(New York: Hopkins, 1802), pp. 25, 33.

AMERICA'S DOMINANT ROLE in preserving peace in Europe can no longer be taken for granted. The need for an extra-regional guarantor has waned, Asia's security problems are likely to be more pressing than those in Europe, and the appetite of the American public for sustained engagement abroad has decreased and may well diminish even further. Although most observers agree that the transatlantic security link is past its heyday, no consensus has emerged about what to do about it. In the preceding chapter, Stephen Walt argues that the transatlantic community should simply scale back its expectations and hope for the best. The dictates of a competitive international system preclude doing more. In the chapter that follows, Charles Kupchan proposes reviving the Atlantic link by deepening its economic and political dimensions while recognizing that the strategic bond will of necessity weaken. The dictates of a competitive international system necessitate institutional efforts to lock in an Atlantic community at peace.

In this chapter I contend that European security depends much more on what happens inside Europe than on what happens between Europe and the United States. Indeed, the only viable solution for ensuring a durable peace in Europe is to end its strategic dependence on the United States and replace it with a political construct capable of preserving stability on its own. Contrary to conventional wisdom, Europe is already well on its way toward erecting such a self-sustaining security order. Integration is the chief mechanism providing order and stability in Europe. Although it has gone largely unnoticed, the European Union is Europe's most important security institution. The continent's long-term stability depends first and foremost on the trajectory of Europe's own process of internal integration.

The case for "integration as security" rests on two central arguments. First, it is the *process* of integration, not its outcome, that is the most important peace-causing effect of the European enterprise. The ongoing process of integration allows individual nation-states to craft national identities wedded to the construction of the new Europe. The interests and identities of individual nation-states become equated with the interests and identities of a broader European polity. Envisaging and participating in the construction of this broader Europe thus becomes an important determinant of domestic legitimacy, ensuring that domestic politics and European politics run on parallel tracks. The individual nation-state is by no means disappearing inside a supranational behemoth, but shared interests and identities allow an arena of postsovereign politics to emerge. The result is a multilayered Europe in which the nation-state and a broader European polity can coexist comfortably. This coexistence is thus contingent on maintaining the political saliency of integration. Were the process of integration to stall or be discredited, individual states would again define their interests and identities in self-referential and competitive terms, and Europe's multilayered construction would come undone.

Second, European integration provides stability not by doing away with geopolitical balancing but by replacing a Europe of many power centers with a Europe of a single center. Many Europeans contend that the European Union (EU) is moving Europe beyond the era of traditional geopolitics; butter is triumphing over guns and cooperation over competition. I disagree. Even if the process of integration continues to thrive, security matters will remain central and their implications potentially hazardous.

The promise of the EU is that it offers a way to channel these security concerns and replace rivalry among competing power centers with cohesion around a single power center, symbolically located in Brussels, but actually in the Franco-German coalition. That a centered Europe already exists is made clear by the fact that a hub-spoke pattern of governance has emerged and by the fact that Europe's core exerts a powerful magnetism over the periphery. The central strategic challenge facing Europe is ensuring the durability of this new political construct consisting of concentric circles around an integral core. Were the process of integration to stall, national identities and interests would come unhinged from those of Europe, and a centered strategic landscape would revert to one of competing poles of power.

As is clear from these introductory remarks, my analysis rests on constructivist foundations. Realists insist that the international system is characterized by an unalterable competitive dynamic. In contrast, constructivists contend that national identities and the rules of the international system are socially constructed; self-regarding states and competitive systems can therefore give way to more collective and cooperative alternatives. Because of their belief in the possibilities of a more cooperative world, constructivists are often portrayed as optimists and realists as pessimists.[1] I want to stress that I do not share the optimism often attributed to the constructivist camp. Indeed, my analysis is quite alarmist in the emphasis it places on the contingent and fragile character of European integration and stability. Integration does provide a pathway for leading to a durable peace in Europe, but sustaining the European project will be no easy task. Americans and Europeans alike need to appreciate

---

1. Alexander Wendt, "Anarchy Is What States Make of It: The Social Construction of Power Politics," *International Organization*, vol. 46, no. 2 (1992), pp. 391–426. For a critique that assumes that constructivism and critical theory necessarily play this political part, see John Mearsheimer, "The False Promise of International Institutions," *International Security*, vol. 19, no. 3 (Winter 1994/95), pp. 5–49, with comments by Keohane and Martin, Kupchan and Kupchan, Ruggie, Wendt, and a reply by Mearsheimer in vol. 20, no. 1 (Summer 1995).

the importance of the European enterprise, recognize the obstacles ahead, and be aware of the high costs of its failure.

National Identity and Foreign Policy

The development of a peaceful Europe ultimately depends on the willingness of major European powers—France and Germany in particular—to continue making European integration a top political priority. Doing so in turn depends on keeping the construction of Europe at the center of domestic political debate and identity formation in individual nation-states. For this, the process of integration must move forward and remain vital enough to motivate and infuse politics at the national level.

Europe is so important precisely because it shapes the national sense of self: what is defined as in "our" interest is highly dependent on who "we" are. Decades of economic integration and efforts to construct a collective political space have succeeded in creating a nascent European polity, which in turn infuses the identity of national states and shapes how those states define their national interests. The practice of close political and economic cooperation has been bolstered by a host of mechanisms created to craft a common European identity, such as a European parliament, flag, currency, and passport, as well as educational and cultural exchanges.[2] By changing notions of "self," the European project has changed old notions of "self-interest" and, consequently, the behavior of individual states. The key is not, as conventional wisdom claims, creating a supranational political space and accompanying images and symbols that succeed in sublimating the national state.[3] Instead, it is crafting identities and interests within individual states that tie national politics to the process of reconstructing Europe. Politics at the national level become so intimately connected to the politics of Europe that the distinction between the two political realms blurs. *The* central challenge facing European statesmen is thus presenting a narrative of the process

2. For discussion of the Europeanization of national identity and its manifestations, see Peter J. Katzenstein, "United Germany in an Integrating Europe," in Peter J. Katzenstein, ed., *Tamed Power: Germany in Europe* (Cornell University Press, 1997), pp. 19–33.

3. Anthony D. Smith, "National Identity and the Idea of European Unity," *International Affairs*, vol. 68, no. 1 (January 1992), pp. 55–76.

of integration that at once resonates with the distinctive historical and cultural needs of each domestic polity and weds the interests and identity of that polity to the construction of Europe.[4]

Since the fall of the Berlin Wall, elites have generated a host of narratives about the European enterprise in order to link national politics to the process of integration.[5] Each major player has come up with its own interpretation—one suited to the idiosyncratic needs of domestic politics. For France, Europe has come to replace the national state as the vehicle for attaining global status and reach. Europe is to do for France what the national state is now too weak to accomplish on its own.[6] For

---

4. Paul Ricoeur, "Reflections on a New Ethos for Europe," *Philosophy & Social Criticism*, vol. 12, no. 5–6 (1995), pp. 3–14; Jerome Brunner, "The Narrative Construction of Reality," *Critical Inquiry*, vol. 18, no. 2 (1991), pp. 1–21.

5. Ole Wæver, "Three Competing Europes: German, French, Russian," *International Affairs*, vol. 66, no. 3 (July 1990), pp. 477–93. More extensively on France and Germany in O. Wæver, U. Holm, and H. Larsen, *The Struggle for "Europe": French and German Concepts of State, Nation and European Union* (forthcoming).

6. A substantial literature is emerging on the interplay among domestic politics, national identity, and foreign policy following this specific approach. On France: Ulla Holm, *Det Franske Europe* (The French Europe) (Århus: Århus Universitetsforlag, 1992); Holm, "The French Garden Is Not What It Used to Be," in Knud-Erik Jørgensen, *Reflective Approaches to European Governance* (London: Macmillan 1997), pp. 128–45; Wæver and others, *The Struggle for "Europe."* On Germany: Wæver and others, *The Struggle for "Europe"*; and Ole Wæver, "Hvordan det hele alligevel kan gå galt . . . ," in Henning Gottlieb and Frede P. Jensen, eds., *Tyskland i Europa* (Copenhagen: SNU, 1995), pp. 297–336; and "Discourse Analysis as Foreign Policy Theory: The Case of Germany and Europe," Working Paper 8.5, University of California at Berkeley, Center for German and European Studies, 1997. On Russia: Iver B. Neumann, *Russian Debates about Europe, 1800–1991*, D.Phil. at Oxford 1992, published as *Russia and the Idea of Europe* (Routledge, 1996). On Turkey: Işil Kazan, "Omvendt Osmannisme og Khanaternes Kemalisme," M.A. thesis (Copenhagen, 1994); Isil Kazan and Ole Wæver, 'Tyrkiet mellem Europa og europæisering,' in *Internasjonal Politikk*, vol. 52, no. 1 (1994); Ayse Kadayifei, "Discourse Analysis and Conflict: Turkish Identity Creation," Ph.D. thesis, University of Kent at Canterbury 1996. On Finland: Pertti Joenniemi, "Euro-Suomi: rajalla, rajojen, valissa vai rajaton?" in Pertti Joenniemi, Risto Alapuro, and Kyösti Pekonen, "Suomesta Euro-Suomen: Keitä me olemme ja mihin matkalla," Occasional Paper 53, Tampere Peace Research Institute, 1993, pp. 13–48. On the United Kingdom: Henrik Larsen, *Discourse Analysis and Foreign Policy* (London: Routledge, 1998); and Thomas Diez, "Reading the EU: Discursive Nodal Points in the British Debate on European Integration," unpublished 1996. On Egypt and India: Sanjoy Banerjee, "National Identity and Foreign Policy," unpublished; Sanjoy Banerjee, "The Cultural Logic of National Identity Formation: Contending Discourses in Late Colonial India," in Valerie M. Hudson, ed., *Culture and Foreign Policy* (Boulder, Colo.: Lynne Rienner, 1997), pp. 27–44. On Slovenia: Lene Hansen, "Slovenian Identity: State Building on the Balkan Border," in *Alternatives*, vol. 21, no. 4 (1996), pp. 473–96. On Greece: Helle Stauersbøll, M.A. in preparation. On the Nordic countries: Lene Hansen and Ole Wæver,

Russia, Europe has come to mean a framework for forging a pan-European political space—one loose enough and wide enough to incorporate Russia itself.[7] And Germany has cast Europe largely as a vehicle for escaping Europe's past by embedding the national state in a larger corporate structure and identity.[8]

These different conceptions of Europe have unfolded simultaneously since 1990. They are competitive, but they are not incompatible. Indeed, that the major states have generated different narratives about Europe facilitates rather than impedes the process of integration. In light of the different domestic needs being fulfilled in the construction of Europe, forcing the major states to agree on a common conception of the enterprise could lead to its unraveling. Each country can, should, and does sustain is own narrative about the project of building the new Europe.

From this perspective, the future of Europe depends less on relations among the major powers than on struggles over the connection between national identity and the European enterprise taking place within key states. As one astute commentator put it, "The struggle for Europe begins with a struggle inside each nation."[9] Unpacking how integration plays domestically in Europe's two key players—Germany and France—is therefore essential to understanding Europe and the challenges it will face in the years ahead. This inquiry in turn leads to the surprising conclusion that Europe has much more of a French problem than a German one.

A dominant German narrative about the European enterprise took shape during the early cold war years and has demonstrated remarkable durability. As Germany became more deeply integrated into Europe and the Atlantic community, German elites sought to reconstruct its national identity so as to equate German self-interest with a broader

---

eds., *Between Nations and Europe: The Political Construction of "Norden" in Finland, Norway, Sweden, and Denmark* (forthcoming). On the United States (as European power): Jesper Møller Sørensen, "The Coming Hegemony? A Constructivist Interpretation of the Future Direction of the U.S. Security Role in Europe," M.A. thesis (Copenhagen 1998). On the United States as global power: John G. Ruggie, "The Past as Prologue? Interests, Identity, and American Foreign Policy," *International Security*, vol. 21, no. 4 (1997), pp. 89–125.

7. Alexei G. Arbatov, "Russia's Foreign Policy Alternatives," *International Security*, vol. 18, no. 2 (1993), pp. 5–43. Compare Neumann, *Russia and the Idea of Europe.*

8. Ole Wæver, "Three Competing Europes. More extensively on France and Germany in Wæver, Holm, and Larsen, *The Struggle for "Europe."*

9. Etienne Tassin, "Europe: A Political Community?" in Chantal Mouffe, ed., *Dimensions of Radical Democracy: Pluralism, Citizenship, Community* (London: Verso, 1992), p. 189.

European and Atlantic self-interest. They succeeded. German policy by the 1980s, in the words of Peter Katzenstein, "reflected German interests. But those interests, pursued through power and bargaining, were fundamentally shaped by the institutional context of Europe and the Europeanization of the identity of the German state that had taken place in the preceding decades."[10] As part of this narrative, the powerful national state was transformed from a concept of promise into one of peril. The concentration of power in the state and the projection of state power externally were both to be avoided. Otherwise, Europe would again fall prey to rivalry among competing power centers, and Germany would be left to fend for itself in an unstable and uncertain landscape.

Since the cold war's end, alternative narratives have emerged in Germany, including those containing a more nationalistic, and less European, vision of Germany and its optimal foreign policy. Some commentators have also articulated what is essentially a neostatist rather than neonationalist argument—that Germany should play the role of a great power just like others have done and will continue to do. But none of these alternative narratives has yet managed to challenge the dominant vision of Europe as a means of rendering benign both the nation and the state. Across the mainstream political parties, integration continues to be viewed primarily as a means of escaping the past.[11]

Many areas of contention do exist between the current Christian Democratic government and the Social Democratic and Green opposition parties. But the parties close ranks when it comes to European integration and the importance of blurring the distinction between European and German interests as a means of preventing return to a continent of aggressively competing national states. The Social Democrats and the Greens emphasize Germany's guilt about World War II and the Holocaust in building the case against the nation-state and power politics. Chancellor Helmut Kohl tends to emphasize geopolitics: a balance-of-power Europe ultimately means the formation of anti-German alliances

10. Katzenstein, "United Germany in an Integrating Europe," p. 15.

11. On the evolution of the European idea as a revolt against Europe's own past, Pim den Boer, Peter Bugge, and Ole Wæver, *The History of the Idea of Europe*, vol. 1 in the series *What Is Europe*, edited by Kevin Wilson and Jan den Dussen; Milton Keynes, *Open University 1993* (commercial republication by Routledge 1995), pp. 151–53, 174; Walter Lipgens, *Europa-Föderationspläne der Widerstandsbewegungen 1940–45* (Munich: Schriften des Forschungsinstituts der deutschen Gesellschaft für Auswärtige Politik, no. 26, 1968); Jean Monnet, *Memoirs* (Doubleday, 1978).

and ongoing destructive rivalries.[12] But both narratives put European integration at the center of German politics and identity and fuel ongoing efforts to embed the German state in a broader European polity.

The unity and consistency of the German narrative on Europe makes that narrative dependent on only one condition: that the larger process of integration continue. A federal Europe need not be at hand. Indeed, it is the act of working on the European project, not arriving at a particular end point or realizing a particular vision, that makes the German narrative viable. In this sense, monetary union is an important hurdle not because of the political and economic implications of a single currency, but because introducing a single currency is for now the centerpiece of the process of integration. The failure of monetary union would thus constitute a broader failure of the European project. As mentioned above, alternative narratives of Germany's place in Europe already exist and are set to become more compelling if integration stalls. But as long as the German polity is actively engaged in building this new Europe, and as long as its identity is linked to whatever political space results, Europe will not have a German problem.

France's narrative about Europe is more fragile and problematic than Germany's for two reasons. First, no single narrative dominates the link between French domestic politics and Europe as it does in Germany. Second, the viability of France's narrative is more dependent on outcomes than on process, thus making it more vulnerable.

Three competing narratives have dominated French debate about Europe since the close of World War II. All of them share a common approach to defining the nation-state, but each rests on a different conception of the relationship between the French nation-state and Europe. These three narratives are: (1) Europe is the arena in which a strong France asserts its autonomy and power (former president Charles de Gaulle); (2) Europe is the vehicle through which a statist (but geopolitically weak) France asserts itself because France can no longer project sufficient influence on its own (former president François Mitterrand); and (3) Europe is the vehicle for creating a federal structure in which the French nation-state loses its saliency, but France is compensated because Europe in return emerges as a formidable global power in a manner resembling the

---

12. Michael Stürmer, *Dissonanzen des Fortschritts: Essays über Geschichte und Politik in Deutschland* (München/Zürich: Piper 1986); Hans-Peter Schwarz, *Die Zentralmacht Europas: Deutschlands Rückkehr auf die Weltbühne* (Berlin: Siedler Verlag, 1994).

French state (former president Valéry Giscard d'Estaing). Although these three narratives emerged at different periods and under different conditions, they have become a central feature of domestic debate in France and of a continuing political struggle over the relationship of the French state to the European enterprise.[13]

The cold war's end intensified this struggle among France's three competing narratives. In the early 1990s, an intermingling of Mitterrand's and Giscard's visions of Europe produced a strong pro-integration orientation. However, the lead-up to the 1992 Maastricht referendum and the narrow margin of victory effectively marginalized Giscard's notion of federalism. Since Maastricht, Mitterrand's vision of Europe and more Gaullist strains have vied for the upper hand, with no clear winner. The absence of a consensus meant that France brought no guiding vision to the Inter-Governmental Conference that began in 1996. As a result, virtually no progress was made on the key issues of institutional reform, enlargement, and development of the WEU. The current cohabitation government of Lionel Jospin and Jacques Chirac has succeeded in maintaining a united front on the importance of making sure that France qualifies for monetary union, but efforts to forge a coherent approach to other aspects of the European agenda have stalled.

Should French elites be unable to articulate a narrative about France's connection to Europe that resonates across the political spectrum, the demands of domestic politics are likely to come into conflict with the demands of Europe. High unemployment and slow growth further complicate the task of sustaining a Europe-oriented foreign policy. Furthermore, all three of the narratives that have shaped French identity and its connection to Europe envisage a particular outcome, not just a process. And this outcome entails strengthening and projecting the power and status of France or Europe—ends that may prove unattainable for some time to come in light of the continent's economic problems and Europe's inability to forge a common defense policy. Even if France's political elites succeed in agreeing on a single narrative about Europe, it may be one that proves unsustainable in a broader European context.

Awareness of the vulnerability of the French narrative about Europe suggests that Germans, British, Americans, and other influential Western actors may want to take deliberate steps to enable France to realize some aspects of its European vision. Whether giving the Western Euro-

---

13. See Holm, *Det Franske Europa.*

pean Union (WEU) more visibility, endowing Europeans with greater influence within NATO's command structure, or granting Europe a greater role in the Middle East peace process, helping France realize its narrative may prove essential to keeping integration on track.

Were French domestic politics to necessitate a turn away from Europe, France would not be the only country to fall off the path of integration. Germany's overall concept of Europe—and of itself—is intimately connected to the viability of the Franco-German coalition. Germany's own narrative about Europe would not last long if its partnership with France unraveled. Europe does not in an immediate sense have a German problem, but it does have a French problem. And the French problem will of necessity bring about a German problem, if not attended to. These domestic struggles over the meaning of "state," "nation," and "Europe" will be the key determinants of Europe's stability in the years ahead.

Europe and Its Three Security Functions

Thus far I have focused on the role that integration has played in refashioning concepts of state and nation and in crafting national identities that wed domestic legitimacy to the enterprise of rebuilding Europe. I do not, however, believe that Europe, as a result of decades of economic integration, is making geopolitics obsolete or is enabling its states to dismiss security competition as a historical artifact. Instead of banishing geopolitical forces from the continent, Europe is seeking to harness them and tap their stabilizing potential. Indeed, it is its ability to link identity, integration, and security that makes the European Union (EU) the most important security institution in Europe.[14]

The EU produces security through three discrete mechanisms. First, the process of integration is replacing a Europe of many centers with a Europe of a single center. Before 1945, each of Europe's major national states constituted an independent center of power. Fragmentation and conflict resulted from competition among these poles. Integration and the establishment of the Franco-German coalition have created a single center. France and Germany retain separate national governments and capitals, but they also engage in practices—joint decisionmaking, a single

14. Ole Wæver, "Identity, Integration and Security: Solving the Sovereignty Puzzle in E.U. Studies," *Journal of International Affairs*, vol. 48, no. 2 (winter 1995), pp. 389–431.

market and currency, joint armed forces—that pool sovereignty and effectively endow Europe with a single power center. Indeed, most of Europe's major initiatives have emerged as the product of the dialogue between and the joint efforts of Paris and Bonn. This gradual process of centering has replaced the fragmentation associated with multipolar competition with a cohesion resulting from Europe's new core-periphery structure. The competitive jockeying of past centuries has given way to a stability engendered by a centered geopolitical formation. In short, the process of integration has succeeded in transforming Europe from a balance-of-power setting to a neoimperial structure.[15]

The geopolitical centering of Europe has transformed its political, economic, and strategic landscape. In terms of both trade and governance, the Franco-German coalition has established a hub-spoke pattern of relations with Europe's smaller powers. These smaller powers have in turn arrayed themselves in concentric circles around the Franco-German core, with each circle trying to move closer to the center. Existing EU members are straining to ensure that they are not left behind by monetary union or excluded from Europe's evolving inner circle.[16] Poland, Hungary, the Czech Republic, and a host of other states are waiting impatiently to become the EU's new outer circle. And others are waiting just to have the opportunity to seek admission. The forces of fragmentation and competition associated with a multipolar Europe have given way to the forces of unification and cooperation associated with a centered Europe.

The EU's second security function follows logically. The EU not only acts as a magnet, pulling Europe's periphery toward its center, but it also induces the periphery to resolve preemptively issues that would otherwise be likely to produce security competition. In this sense, the

15. Adam Watson, *The Evolution of International Society* (London: Routledge, 1993); Ole Wæver, "Europe's Three Empires: A Watsonian Interpretation of Post-Wall European Security," in Rick Fawn and Jeremy Larkins, eds., *International Society after the Cold War: Anarchy and Order Reconsidered* (London: Macmillan in association with Millennium, 1996), pp. 220–60; Charles Kupchan, "After Pax Americana: Benign Power, Regional Integration, and the Sources of a Stable Multipolarity," *International Security*, vol. 23, no. 2 (fall 1998).

16. Sweden, for example, is concerned about being too far from Europe's center, while Denmark is concerned about being too close—one of the reasons for Denmark's initial rejection of the Maastricht Treaty. See Ole Wæver, "Nordic Nostalgia: Northern Europe after the Cold War," *International Affairs*, vol. 68, no.1 (January 1992), pp. 77–102; Hans Mouritzen, "The Nordic Model as a Foreign Policy Instrument: Its Rise and Fall," *Journal of Peace Research*, vol. 32, no.1, pp. 45–59.

EU exercises a silent discipline in those parts of Europe most prone to conflict. Prospective entrants into the club are well aware that they must adhere to certain standards of behavior (on issues such as democratization, privatization, treatment of minorities, handling of border disputes) if they are to gain membership. The allure of entry has thus far proved sufficiently strong to induce Europe's new democracies to adhere to these standards. Czechs and Slovaks made sure that their divorce occurred in a fashion consistent with EU standards.[17] The prospect of membership also played an important role in inducing Hungary and Romania to reach an agreement on long-standing border and minority issues. So too has this silent disciplining been operating in the Baltics, putting pressure on governments to avoid discrimination against Russian minorities.

By creating incentives for Europe's new democracies to resolve disputes that would otherwise fester, the EU effectively preempts potential sources of conflict. Like its centering function, this disciplining of the periphery occurs silently and invisibly, without resort to the traditional instrument of security policy—the use (or threat of use) of military force. Its novel approach to promoting stability does not, however, minimize its effects. By doing away with multipolar balancing and encouraging the new democracies to resolve disputes before they escalate, the EU is having a profound impact on Europe's strategic landscape.

The EU's third security function is that of playing a more traditional military role. Curiously, it is in the military realm that the EU's security role is the weakest. The WEU remains a nascent security organization. Its role in Bosnia has been quite limited. To the extent that Europeans resort to the use of military force, they do so largely through NATO and under the guise of American leadership.

The absence of a greater EU role in traditional military matters is not that puzzling or troubling, however, when viewed in the context of the link that exists between domestic politics and the construction of Europe. That the EU contributes to security in Europe largely through the two functions just outlined rather than through coordinating deterrence and military action stems from the fact that European publics see the past—not Russian troops, Balkan nationalism, or Islamic fundamentalism—as the main threat to their well-being. Since the end of World War II, the idea of Europe has to a large extent been cast as a revolt against

17. Jiri Pehe, "Czechs and Slovaks Define Postdivorce Relations," RFE/RL Research Report (Radio Free Europe/Radio Liberty), vol. 1, no. 45 (November 13, 1992), pp. 7–11.

Europe's bloody history.[18] This narrative has resonated strongly among generations of Europeans who lived through World War II and the rebuilding of Europe. Except in France, where the projection of power and influence has been a part of the domestic narrative about the construction of Europe, the absence of a more robust military dimension to the European enterprise strengthens, and does not undermine, the critical link between domestic identity and integration.

Generational change does raise troubling questions about the sustainability of this narrative over the long run. For younger generations that did not live through World War II or the rebuilding of Europe, fear of the past will serve as a less potent narrative justifying integration. Even in Germany, sustaining momentum behind the European enterprise may entail a greater role for Europe in managing traditional military security. Such a shift would also ease the task of legitimating Europe within the confines of France's domestic political debate. Concern about these issues is one reason that European elites are focusing renewed attention on building a more robust common foreign and security policy and pushing forward changes in command structures that will facilitate Europe-only military operations.

Building a more substantial foreign and security policy offers an increasingly attractive alternative to other options for fostering a more developed sense of European identity. On the one hand, efforts to create more cultural uniformity and political centralization (through education policy, cultural exchanges, and the proliferation of supranational institutions) will continue to face resistance at the national level. Efforts to identify a new external enemy—whether it be Islam, a resurgent Russia, or a threat not yet articulated—also promise either to become a self-fulfilling prophecy or to ring hollow. A more active and assertive Europe, on the other hand, promises to enable Europeans to view the EU as a more legitimate target of loyalty and allegiance. Outsiders will also view the EU as a more significant international actor, in turn reinforcing the vital link between domestic politics in EU members and the construction of Europe. Over time, sustaining integration may well necessitate

18. Jean Baudrillard, *The Illusion of the End,* translated by Chris Turner (Stanford University Press, 1992), pp. 32ff; Jacques Derrida, *The Other Heading: Reflections on Today's Europe* (Indiana University Press 1992); Helle Rytkønen, "Securing European Identity—Identifying Danger," paper presented at the annual meeting of the International Studies Association, Chicago, February 1995.

that Europe become an actor on the international scene, not just a political construction that checks intra-European rivalry. In accordance with a strong tradition of European political thought, only by being an international actor does a polity fully come into being.[19]

Even if greater activism in the traditional realm of security affairs does not emerge, the EU, not the North Atlantic Treaty Organization (NATO), will remain Europe's most important security institution. NATO may have control over military assets and command structures, but it is the EU and the process of centered integration that it oversees that are the main sources of European stability. NATO may be keeping the peace in Bosnia, but it is the EU that is keeping the peace in Europe.

NATO and America's Role in a Centered Europe

NATO is enjoying surprising longevity and vitality. It stopped the bloodshed in Bosnia while the initial Europe-only intervention failed to do so. It is proceeding with the admission of new members, enhancing stability in central Europe and ensuring that Germany relies on multilateral institutions to address its security interests in the region. NATO's post–cold war relevance and resiliency have prompted many analysts to praise its virtues and to counsel the EU against taking on a greater defense role or pursuing other policies that might undermine the Western alliance.[20]

19. Werner Hoyer and Michael Barnier (German and French members of the EU's "reflection group" that prepared the IGC-96), "Existiert Europa? Ein deutsch-französischen Plädoyer für eine gemeinsame Aussen- und Sicherheitspolitik," *Frankfurter Allgemeine Zeitung*, December 7, 1995; Marlene Wind ("Eksisterer Europa? Reflektioner over forsvar, identitet og borgerdyd i et nyt Europa," in Christen Sørensen, ed., *Europa Nation-Union— efter Minsk og Maastricht* (København: Fremad, 1992), p. 24), quotes an article by Francois Goguel from *Le Figaro* of April 4, 1991, entitled "Europe does not exist" (reflecting on the feeble appearance of the EU in the Gulf War), and French historian François Furet writes, "Europe now stands at a crossroads, where only by uniting may it still parry its decline. If it cannot accomplish this, the twenty-first century may well take shape without it." "Europe after Utopianism," *Journal of Democracy*, vol. 6, no. 1 (January 1995), p. 89. On changes intended to strengthen the European pillar, Paul Cornish, "European Security: The End of Architecture and the New NATO," *International Affairs*, vol. 72, no. 4 (October 1996), pp. 751–70; John G. Ruggie, "Consolidating the European Pillar: The Key to NATO's Future," *Washington Quarterly*, vol. 20, no. 1 (Winter 1997), pp. 109–24.

20. Compare Charles L. Glaser, "Why NATO Is Still Best: Future Security Arrangements for Europe," *International Security*, vol. 18, no. 1 (Summer 1993), pp. 5–50; Gordon, "Does the WEU Have a Role?"

Nevertheless, there are two reasons to be wary of assessments that put such confidence in NATO. First, although NATO has demonstrated remarkable durability in the absence of a Soviet threat, history and the logic of alliances call into question its ability to remain cohesive and directed. As Stephen Walt argues in his chapter, an alliance is unlikely to survive for long without an enemy against which to balance.[21] NATO may try to transform itself into a collective security organization, embracing not just central Europe, but Russia and former Soviet republics as well. And it may try to become an all-purpose vehicle for coordinating collective military action even well beyond the borders of Europe.[22] But it is by no means clear that the U.S. Congress or its parliamentary counterparts in Europe will go along. NATO may disprove its critics and be around for decades to come. But the fact that grand coalitions usually dissolve when their enemies disappear from the scene warrants prudential preparation for NATO's possible demise.

Second, excessive reliance on NATO risks undermining the EU and standing in the way of the process of integration so central to maintaining the EU's three security functions. A new generation of European elites and voters may well necessitate that the EU develop a more robust defense role to help build a new narrative about integration that resonates with European publics. In this sense, weaning Europe from depending too heavily on American military capability could help build momentum behind the integration process. So too might a Europe that is more influential with respect to east Asia and North America be a more stable and legitimate political construction. For the United States to discourage Europe's further deepening because it might pose a challenge to NATO and come at the expense of transatlantic ties is to overlook the potent stabilizing effects of integration and to jeopardize the most important determinant of peace in Europe. Sustaining the process of integration must be the top priority, even if transatlantic relations and American influence in Europe suffer as a result.

21. Compare Walt's chapter. See also Gunther Hellmann and Reinhard Wolf, "Neorealism, Neoliberal Institutionalism and the Future of NATO," *Security Studies*, vol. 3, no. 1 (Autumn 1993), pp. 3–43.

22. See RAND study by Ronald D. Asmus, Richard L. Kugler, and F. Stephen Larrabee published as "Building a New NATO," *Foreign Affairs*, vol. 72, no. 4 (September/October 1993), pp. 28–40, and abbreviated as "It's Time for a New U.S.-European Strategic Bargain," *International Herald Tribune*, August 28–29, 1993, p. 6. See their continued elaborations in *Survival*, vol. 37, no. 1 (Spring 1995), and *Washington Quarterly*, vol. 19, no. 2 (Spring 1996).

This analysis leads to the conclusion that NATO should by all means be preserved if possible, but that its well-being should not come at the expense of further European integration. NATO still provides the military hardware and command structures needed for coordinated operations. It maintains a strategic link across the Atlantic that facilitates close political cooperation between Europe and the United States. And it keeps U.S. forces in Europe, providing an insurance-like deterrent and enabling the EU to concentrate its attention on political and economic integration.

But to assume that Europe's security must be primarily dependent on NATO is to misread Europe and to lead policymakers to dangerous conclusions. To cling to NATO even if doing so compromises the European enterprise will leave the alliance hollow and prone to unraveling from within. In the absence of an external threat, NATO needs the EU to prevent the return of intra-European rivalries, not vice versa. Subsuming the EU in a broader Atlantic union, as Charles Kupchan suggests in chapter 4, may solidify the transatlantic link and keep the United States in Europe. But because it would dilute and jeopardize the European enterprise and impede the main sources of stability in Europe—integration and the creation of a centered Europe—an Atlantic union risks precipitating the unraveling of Europe that Kupchan is seeking to avoid.

Conclusion

Because this chapter rests on somewhat unorthodox arguments, I will conclude by summarizing how my views diverge from more traditional analyses of European security. I identify four hypotheses that have become part of the conventional wisdom, and then offer my own interpretation.

(1) *Conventional Wisdom:* Loyalty to Europe's nation-states continues to overshadow loyalty to Europe. Therefore, the nation-state is here to stay, integration will stall, and a common foreign and security policy will not emerge.

> *My interpretation:* The process of integration has transformed the interests and identities of Europe's individual states, linking domestic legitimacy to the construction of a new Europe. As a result, loyalty to the nation-state is compatible with loyalty to Europe.

(2) *Conventional Wisdom:* Either realists à la Walt are right and Europe will return to the rivalries of the inter-war period, or liberals à la Kupchan are right and democracy and deeper social transformation will take us beyond geopolitics and security competition.

> *My interpretation:* Balancing, security competition, and geopolitics will not go away, but they can be refashioned by the process of European integration. Europe is today held together not by the democratic peace, but by a centered geopolitical structure that pulls the periphery toward the core. Europe's strategic landscape resembles an empire, a formation with a long track record of providing stability.

(3) *Conventional Wisdom:* The unraveling of the transatlantic alliance represents the most serious threat to European security. It would precipitate the renationalization of defense policies within Europe and trigger a return to competitive balancing.

> *My interpretation:* The most serious threat to European security arises from the possibility that narratives about the construction of Europe no longer resonate domestically, causing major states to diverge from the path of integration. Europe's principal "other" is still its own past, providing a steady impetus behind integration. But generational change may require recasting the critical connection between national identity and the European enterprise. This recasting may necessitate that Europe take on greater military responsibilities and seek to project influence in other regions.

(4) *Conventional Wisdom:* In the aftermath of the cold war, the weakening of the strategic link between Europe and North America necessitates political and economic initiatives (such as an Atlantic union or a free trade zone) to rejuvenate the transatlantic partnership. The bloc-based protectionism currently practiced by the European Union will, on the other hand, erode transatlantic cohesion.

> *My interpretation:* Attempts to create an Atlantic union or free trade zone would damage transatlantic relations by triggering European opposition and by undermining the process of intraregional integration in Europe. Solidifying integration in-

side Europe must take precedence over solidifying integration across the Atlantic.

Because conventional wisdom presents an inaccurate assessment of the sources of peace in Europe, mainstream analysts and policymakers are pursuing counterproductive initiatives for responding to a new strategic landscape. They are right in saying that transatlantic relations are likely to suffer from the disappearance of the Soviet Union, but they are wrong to argue that the solution is to look for new ways to interpose America in Europe's evolving political and economic construction. The EU is Europe's most important security institution precisely because it is *European*, and it provides a way for Europe to escape a return to its past. Yes, a single currency and a more inward-looking Europe might come at the expense of transatlantic economic ties. And yes, a stronger European defense identity might diminish the prominence of NATO and help Europe, as opposed to the collective West, take on a more global role. But if these developments strengthen the European enterprise and enable integration to proceed apace, then they will in the long run make peace in Europe more durable. Even if transatlantic relations suffer in the process, the United States will benefit from a Europe that is both at peace and a more cohesive and coherent partner.

If, on the other hand, the United States presses for NATO's preeminence, argues for the establishment of an Atlantic union or free trade zone, and opposes efforts to forge a common European defense policy, it risks not just straining ties across the Atlantic, but also jeopardizing the process of integration that must move forward if Europe is to remain free of security competition among its key states. American policy would in the first instance provoke the opposition of France (which still wants the Americans in militarily but out politically) and other EU members committed to deeper *European* integration. But of greater consequence in the long run would be America's adulteration of Europe's experiment with a new pathway to peace—one that replaces a Europe of competing poles of power with a Europe of a single center and a core-periphery structure that induces cohesion and cooperation. The EU's critical role in bringing peace to Europe may go largely unnoticed because it acts invisibly and silently, without the fanfare and hardware of NATO. But to overlook its quiet peace-causing effects is to ignore the most important determinant of stability in Europe.

During the cold war, getting transatlantic relations right was the top priority and the key to peace on the continent. European integration followed. During the current era, getting Europe right is the top priority and the key to peace on the continent. The transatlantic relationship matters, but it will be determined by, rather than determine, what happens inside Europe and whether Europe's own attempt to escape its past proves successful.

Chapter 4

Reconstructing the West
The Case for an Atlantic Union

Charles A. Kupchan

T HE WEST has cause to rejoice as this century draws to a close. The fundamental ideological and geopolitical cleavages of past decades are no longer. Democracy and capitalism have triumphed over fascism and communism, and this era's three revisionist states— Germany, Japan, and Russia—are quiescent. Disputes that festered for decades in the Middle East, Africa, and Latin America are moving toward resolution. And the world economy is growing more liberal and more vibrant as old markets expand and new ones come on line.

But the success of the West may also become its undoing. North America and Europe risk drifting apart in the absence of the geopolitical imperative that brought them together. Domestic priorities have stolen the limelight from foreign policy as electorates in the Western democracies turn inward. Asia's economic woes and political volatility will increasingly attract U.S. resources and attention, at least to some extent at the expense of the transatlantic link. Even the cultural affinity enjoyed by Americans and Europeans will weaken as populations on both sides of the Atlantic become more diverse.

Aware of these challenges, American and European leaders are seeking to breathe new life into the Atlantic community. They have justifiably resisted calls to revitalize the West by identifying a new enemy—whether it be Islam, Orthodox Christianity, a rising China, or poverty and chaos in the underdeveloped world. Instead, policymakers are seeking to bind together the democracies of America and Europe by deepening and broadening the institutions that served the Atlantic community so well during the cold war. The European Union (EU) is persisting in its quest for a federal Europe while at the same time opening its doors to the continent's new democracies. The borders of the North Atlantic Treaty Organization (NATO) are expected to expand eastward as well, ensuring America's engagement in Europe and defending an enlarged community of democracies.

Yet despite their good intentions, the leaders of the established democracies have embarked on a course that will lead to the demise of the West, not its renewal. The core of the problem is that they are trying to broaden the community of peaceful, democratic nations even as they deepen it. But they must first loosen the West's structures if enlargement is to be both politically feasible and strategically desirable.

In the absence of the Soviet threat, the vision of Europe embodied in the Maastricht Treaty is now but a legacy of a former era. Preparations for monetary union notwithstanding, efforts to move toward centralized governance of Europe and a common foreign and security policy are foundering as national states dig in and resist further attempts to whittle away their sovereignty.[1] Worse still, the futile push toward federalism is absorbing the energy and resources that should be devoted to the EU's most important and urgent mission: its enlargement to the east.[2]

NATO, at the same time, is addressing the task of enlargement with the urgency it deserves. But NATO is misdirecting its energies into a heated debate over which central European countries to admit and when to do so, failing to recognize that the problem is in the very nature of the alliance, not its membership. Formal military blocs and the rigor of territorial guarantees are no longer necessary or politically sustainable. Rather than asking "who gets in when?" NATO should be asking "what are they getting into?"

---

1. The 1996–1997 Intergovernmental Conference in Turin made clear that Europe is falling far short of many of the objectives laid out in the Maastricht Treaty. It failed to produce significant progress on key issues such as institutional reform and a common foreign and security policy.

2. EU officials argue that Europe's internal construction must be settled before it proceeds with taking in new members. See, for example, "Reinforcing Political Union and Preparing for Enlargement," Official Commission Opinion, February 28, 1996, prepared for the Intergovernmental Conference in Turin. I accept that some institutional change—in particular, reform of voting rules and of agricultural and regional assistance policies—is needed to pave the way for enlargement. But, for reasons outlined in this chapter, I challenge the general proposition that deepening needs to precede or even accompany widening.

Unless the EU and NATO undertake fundamental reform, they risk coming apart just as they draw within reach of completing their historic mission to unite a peaceful and democratic Europe. The excessive ambition of current policies will overextend Western institutions, undermining the transatlantic community as member states defect from unwanted commitments. Instead, Western leaders must scale back their vision and seek to strike a balance between institutions that demand too much and those that deliver too little. They must devise a framework that occupies a new and vital center and that promises to match commitments and responsibilities to political realities.

The solution to the West's dilemmas is an Atlantic union (AU) that would subsume the EU and NATO. The EU would abandon its federal aspirations and concentrate instead on the extension of its single market east to central Europe and west to North America. NATO would become the defense arm of the AU, but its binding commitments to the collective defense of state borders would give way to more relaxed commitments to uphold collective security through peace enforcement, peacekeeping, and preventive diplomacy. The AU could then open its doors to the new democracies of central Europe in a manner acceptable to both Russia and commitment-weary electorates in NATO countries. Once democracy took root in Russia and other states of the former Soviet Union, the AU would include them in its security structures and single market. Institutions that promote civic engagement and legislative oversight at the transatlantic level should be created to undergird and legitimate an Atlantic union of democratic states.

An AU would sacrifice depth for breadth. But a looser and more comprehensive transatlantic union would ensure that the bridge between North America and an enlarged Europe rests on solid economic and political trestles, not just on increasingly weak strategic ones. It would thus lock in, and eventually extend, perhaps the most profound transformation of our century: the creation of a community of democratic nation-states among which war has become unthinkable. The Western democracies have built much more than an alliance of convenience among countries that are each out for individual gain. They enjoy unprecedented levels of trust and reciprocity and share a political order based on capitalist economies and liberal societies.[3] The consolidation

3. See Daniel Deudney and G. John Ikenberry, "The Logic of the West," *World Policy Journal* (Winter 1993/94), pp. 17–25.

and expansion of this democratic core hold the greatest promise for a stable peace in the Atlantic region and beyond and offer a sensible and prudent starting point as the United States casts about for a new grand strategy.

Theoretical Foundations

To provide a foundation for the policy analysis that follows and to sharpen the contrast between my analysis and that found in chapters 2 (by Stephen Walt) and 3 (by Ole Wæver), I begin by making clear my main theoretical assumptions. As stated in the introduction, my analysis occupies a middle ground, seeking to bridge Walt's concern with power and polarity and Wæver's concern with identity. I take international structure, as defined by the location and relative strength of geographic concentrations of power, as an important determinant of state behavior.[4] Accordingly, the collapse of the Soviet Union, the deterioration of Russia's economy and armed forces, and the consequent disappearance of the West's principal external threat will ultimately have a powerful effect on the tenor of U.S.-European relations. Structural considerations alone are insufficient to predict what will become of the transatlantic community, but they do provide good reason to believe that this community will be looser and less cohesive than it was during the cold war. In the absence of a unifying external threat, neither Europe nor the bridge between Europe and America will be able to bear as much weight as they did during past decades. This structural argument is the basis for my skepticism about the current course of policy and the proposition that NATO and the EU will not just survive this period of transition, but become both deeper and broader. Structural change does not mandate that Western institutions should collapse, only that they should be less ambitious in terms of the functions they fulfill and the sacrifices they demand from member states.

Structure and polarity do matter; it is misleading to conceive of a uniform international arena that operates according to a uniform structural logic. Indeed, one of the quiet revolutions of the twentieth century has been the carving out of nonanarchic space. Within the community that

4. This assumption is, needless to say, a centerpiece of the realist canon. See chapter 2 for the relevant citations.

68   Charles A. Kupchan

encompasses the Western democracies, the self-help behavior and competitive jockeying that realists associate with anarchy have been all but
eliminated. Neither within Europe nor across the Atlantic does it make
sense to conceive of state-based poles of power that are competing with
each other for dominance. Anarchy and structural polarity have been
moderated by the character of the units wielding power and by the expectations that these units have of one another's behavior.

The creation of this nonanarchic space has been the product of two
separate, but related, processes. On the one hand, institutionalist notions of transparency and reciprocity have gradually deepened cooperation and trust among the Western democracies. Repeated interaction
over time and the proliferation of a thick network of rule-based institutions and associations enable states to expect reciprocity and to pursue
cooperative strategies with little fear of being exploited.[5]

On the other hand, the constructivist account and its focus on identity
capture the extent to which changes in the character and identity of the
relevant actors contribute to the moderation of anarchy.[6] Germans, for
example, have redefined how they conceive of nationhood and the role
of their nation in the international arena.[7] Germany is now a civil power
that willfully binds its coercive potential. It equates its well-being as a
nation-state with the well-being of Europe and its institutions. Europe's
smaller states are now comfortable bandwagoning with rather than balancing against German power precisely because they have noted this
change in national identity and believe that Germany will exercise its
influence in a benign manner.

Changes in national identity affect not just the behavior of states, but
also the depth and character of a supranational political space. It makes
sense to speak of a Western *community* precisely because the Atlantic
democracies share a political space grounded in common values and a
common identity. If national governments and the electorates to whom

5. Some of the main works representing an institutionalist account of cooperation include Robert Keohane, *After Hegemony* (Princeton University Press, 1984); Kenneth Oye,
ed., *Cooperation under Anarchy* (Princeton University Press, 1985); Robert Axelrod, *The
Evolution of Cooperation* (New York: Basic Books, 1984) .

6. See Alexander Wendt, "Anarchy Is What States Make of It," *International Organization*, vol. 46, no. 2 (Spring 1992); and Peter Katzenstein, ed., *The Culture of National Security* (Columbia University Press, 1996).

7. Thomas Berger, "Norms, Identity, and National Security in Germany and France," in
Katzenstein, *The Culture of National Security*, pp. 317–356.

they are beholden at least to some extent affiliate and identify with a Western community of national states, then that political space becomes a legitimate arena of politics and a target of political loyalty. Similarly, the identification of European publics with a European polity makes the EU a legitimate and durable political space. I do not accept Wæver's contention that Europe has entered the era of postsovereignty. The national state is alive and well. Indeed, it is the strength of national loyalty and sovereignty that is preventing Europe from moving more decidedly in the direction of a federal structure. At the same time, EU member states do practice an attenuated form of sovereignty made possible by the existence of shared identity elements. It is this mixture of a shared identity and the attenuation of sovereignty that gives rise to a supranational realm of politics that sits comfortably alongside politics at the national level.[8]

The policy implications of this theoretical construct are as follows. If the transatlantic community is to outlast geopolitical change and remain a pocket of nonanarchic space, it must pursue both institutionalist and constructivist pathways to cooperation. This prognosis means sustaining an institutional context that facilitates concrete acts of cooperation and that promotes transparency and trust. Because the systemic incentives for institutionalized cooperation have diminished, cooperation may be harder to achieve. Institutional structures will need to be adjusted accordingly. And to offset the weakening of these systemic incentives, the Atlantic partners should undertake explicit efforts to deepen a common identity. Promoting a sense of community and commonality will deepen trust, encourage states to define interests in collective rather than solely national terms, and strengthen the legitimacy of a supranational political space.

For the United States, these prescriptions mean finding a formula that keeps America directly involved in managing European security, though at lower cost and with diminished responsibilities. This formula will ultimately entail a more equitable sharing of burdens between the United States and its European partners. It will also entail embedding the strategic aspects of the transatlantic relationship in a broader political and economic framework. In addition, U.S. elites need to use educational

---

8. This notion of national states' transferring some level of identity and loyalty to a supranational space draws on Deutsch's notion of a security community. See Karl Deutsch, *Political Community and the North Atlantic Area* (New York: Greenwood Press, 1969).

initiatives, exchange programs, and transatlantic associations to drive home to Americans that they have an Atlantic calling and that they share a common political space with Europeans.

Europeans need to accept that their vision of "Europe" may have to be scaled back. The success of the EU should be measured in terms of its ability to preserve nonanarchic space, not against some preconceived notion of a federal Europe. From this perspective, too much Europe could be as dangerous as too little. If the EU strives for a level of supranationality that exceeds the tolerance of national electorates, its member states will defect, calling into question not just specific policy measures but the legitimacy of the broader enterprise. The existence of a dominant narrative on where Europe is headed and the notion that integration must keep moving forward therefore stand in the way of the EU's evolution. This narrative of European unity is not, as Wæver concludes, needed to prevent Europe's unraveling. Instead, Europeans must accept that less union may be better than more and that the EU may find a stable resting point that falls well short of what is currently envisioned.

More important than arriving at a vision of Europe's ultimate disposition is consolidating the Franco-German coalition and ensuring that this coalition continues to focus on managing power rather than on aggregating it.[9] Wæver is right in arguing that the Franco-German core endows Europe with characteristics of an empire. This center of power provides leadership and hierarchy within the EU; it is the foundation for the hub-spoke pattern of governance that characterizes relations between Europe's core and periphery. But Wæver is wrong to call for a construction that seeks to establish a unified Europe as a global power. Europe must continue to focus on binding its power and exercising it in partnership with the United States rather than seeking to aggregate its power and project it externally. Otherwise, the EU may find that it enjoys internal cohesion and peace, but at the expense and danger of triggering rivalry with other power centers in Eurasia or North America. Even as Europe becomes a more active partner of the United States in

---

9. The very existence of the Franco-German coalition—and the EU more generally—confounds realist analysis. If Walt, for example, is pessimistic about the integrity of the transatlantic link, why should he not be equally pessimistic about the EU? His chapter suggests a certain optimism about the durability of the union. But a realist perspective would predict the return of national rivalry between France and Germany and the consequent unraveling of the EU.

addressing security affairs both within and outside Europe, the union must remain an instrument for moderating and binding power, not for projecting it.[10]

Preempting Objections

Before proceeding with my analysis of transatlantic security relations, I will preempt two potential objections to the overall enterprise that informs both this essay and this volume more generally. One objection stems from the assertion that the transatlantic relationship is not worth saving because Europe no longer matters sufficiently to American prosperity or security. The other stems from the more dangerous assertion that the problem of preserving the transatlantic community will take care of itself because new external threats are taking shape that will ensure the West's cohesion.

Why Europe Still Matters

Just as Asia-firsters attacked America's Atlanticism during the early post–World War II years, so too they are now arguing that preserving the transatlantic community is not worth the effort.[11] Asia-firsters contend that Atlanticism has served its purpose and that the United States has far more pressing needs at home and in the Pacific. Now that Europe faces only limited threats and isolated conflicts, it no longer requires American attention and resources; Europeans can and should assume responsibility for their own security. Asia is far more deserving

---

10. My opposition to Europe's emergence as a global power stems from two concerns. First, unlike the United States, the EU does not lie between two major oceans. An EU that focuses on aggregating and projecting power rather than on managing it is therefore likely to trigger responsive balancing by other powers on the Eurasian continent. The EU will not have the luxury of acting as an off-shore balancer. Second, the Franco-German coalition acts as a magnet drawing the periphery toward the core largely because the periphery believes that the core will bind itself and exercise its power in a benign manner. Should the Franco-German coalition adopt a different vision of Europe that focuses on maximizing rather than managing power, the periphery is more likely to balance against the core, causing the EU to fragment.

11. For discussion of this earlier debate between Asia-firsters and Europe-firsters, see Jack Snyder, *Myths of Empire* (Cornell University Press, 1991).

of the top spot in America's new geopolitical priorities. It promises to be an engine of global economic growth during the coming century.[12] The United States should therefore be poised to tap into the region's new markets and capital flows. And unstable regional alignments, in combination with uncertainty about how China will cope with its newfound power, necessitate the deterrent and stabilizing effect of a robust American military presence. Asia's ascendance, the argument runs, must signal the end of America's Eurocentrism and the beginning of a grand strategy anchored in the Pacific rather than the Atlantic.

The Pacific Basin's economic potential and political volatility notwithstanding, an Asia-first grand strategy is fundamentally flawed. Europe still matters for three compelling reasons. First, despite the end of the cold war, the U.S.-European partnership continues to serve as the fulcrum for broader multilateral action in the international arena. A transatlantic coalition was behind all the central diplomatic initiatives of this past decade—countering Iraqi aggression in the Persian Gulf, bringing to a successful conclusion the Uruguay Round of trade negotiations, paving the way for a lasting peace in the Middle East, helping to build democracy in the former Soviet bloc, and enforcing the Dayton Accord in Bosnia. In addition, the transatlantic partnership is at the heart of the institutional infrastructure that underpins ongoing efforts to liberalize the international trading system and to prevent and stop conflict. To the extent that a set of norms and rules are gradually becoming embedded in the international system, the driving force emanates from the common values and efforts of the Western democracies. For the foreseeable future, no Asian power or coalition of powers will be able to fill the shoes of America's European allies in helping to construct an international order based on the principles of liberal multilateralism. The United States should by all means sustain a cooperative relationship with Japan and seek to channel China's coming economic and military might toward constructive ends. But a strong Atlantic coalition will enhance, not diminish, American leverage in East Asia.

---

12. Despite East Asia's recent economic troubles, many analysts foresee a return to robust growth for the region. Part of the explanation is east Asia's savings and investment rates, which are roughy fifty percent higher than those in North America and Europe. See Steven Radelet and Jeffrey Sachs, "Asia's Reemergence," *Foreign Affairs*, vol. 76, no. 6 (November/December 1997); and Roger Altman and Charles A. Kupchan, "Arresting the Decline of Europe," *World Policy Journal*, vol. 14, no. 4 (Winter 1997/98).

Second, Europe itself would be deeply unsettled should the Atlantic connection wither and America disengage from the continent. Whether by design or default, NATO has greatly facilitated Europe's coming together by assuming responsibility for hard-core security issues, leaving the European Community (the EU's forebear) free to pursue political and economic integration. As Europe's failure to act decisively and effectively in Bosnia made clear, the EU is not ready to take over the management of European security. Indeed, an American withdrawal would send shock waves across Europe, perhaps threatening even the Franco-German coupling by forcing Germany to reconsider its security needs. Should this unraveling of Europe come about, the bedrock of U.S. foreign policy—a cohesive western Europe at peace—would be shaken loose.

Third, to allow the transatlantic community to erode would be to miss an opportunity to lock in the zone of democratic peace that North America and western Europe have succeeded in constructing. Countries within this zone have all but eliminated the security competition and jockeying for relative advantage that have characterized international politics for millennia. It may be that without a common threat, it will not be long before relations among the Western democracies again fall prey to traditional power balancing and the search for individual gain. But it is worth trying to do better and to make permanent the establishment of a grouping of nations among which war is no more.

The Fallacy of the Rest against the West

The most effective and familiar means of ensuring the vitality of the West would be to find it a new enemy. A transcendent external threat would provide a new "other" against which the Atlantic democracies could renew their common identity and sense of shared purpose. Whether motivated by concern about restoring the West's cohesion or by a sincere assessment that dire threats are looming on the horizon, the search for new fault lines is currently all the rage. Professor Samuel Huntington, for example, sees other civilizations as the new enemy against which America and Europe should gird their loins.[13] Profound cultural differences, Huntington contends, will ultimately lead to a clash of incompat-

13. Samuel Huntington, "The Clash of Civilizations?" *Foreign Affairs*, vol. 72, no. 4 (Summer 1993), pp. 22–49.

ible civilizations. While Huntington sees the most serious threat to the West emanating from a Confucian-Islamic connection, others worry more about a coming divide between Western and Orthodox Christianity.

Robert Kaplan argues that the coming cleavage will fall along socioeconomic rather than civilizational lines. Poverty, illness, and violence in underdeveloped regions promise only to worsen, threatening to engulf the industrialized West. In a variation on the same theme, Matthew Connelly and Paul Kennedy fear overpopulation and migration from the poorer south to the richer north. "Demographic-technological fault lines," they contend, will define the landscape of the twenty-first century.[14] The nations of the wealthy West must now come together to combat poverty and overpopulation lest they be overrun by the world's poor.

These efforts to provide the West with a new mission and raison d'être are dead ends. Ideological and religious affinities do not translate into geopolitical alliance any more than ideological and religious differences necessarily trigger conflict.[15] The Confucian and Islamic worlds—let alone the two together—are hardly coherent political actors; both face tenacious by ethnic, religious, and national divides. And Orthodox Europe is not preparing to do battle with Western Christianity. Former Soviet republics are still in the midst of efforts to reclaim nationhood and rediscover their cultural distinctiveness. But Russia and its neighbors are, for the most part, looking westward with hope, not fear. A new east-west divide in Europe may ultimately take shape, but it should not do so because of a self-fulfilling prophecy set in motion by the West's own actions. The challenge for the West is to live comfortably alongside these other civilizations, not to orchestrate willfully or by accident a collision with them.

Overpopulation and poverty are far more worrisome than trumped-up cultural clashes. Increases in population will put additional strain on the South's already scarce resources. Wealth inequalities between the north and south will widen. But the connection between social breakdowns in, say, sub-Saharan Africa and the well-being of the West is at best tenuous. As they have well demonstrated, the industrialized democracies are very good at tolerating and cordoning off suffering in far-

14. Robert Kaplan, "The Coming Anarchy," *Atlantic Monthly*, vol. 243, no. 2 (February 1994), pp. 44–76; Matthew Connelly and Paul Kennedy, "Must It Be the Rest against the West?" *Atlantic Monthly*, vol. 244, no. 6 (December 1994), p. 76.

15. For evidence that ideological factors are weak determinants of alliance formation, see Stephen Walt, *The Origins of Alliances* (Cornell University Press, 1987).

away places. Efforts to instill public alarm by concocting visions of millions of diseased and dispossessed storming the beaches of New Jersey—or even the Côte d'Azur—are simply too far-fetched. The Western democracies should soberly assess how they might help avoid the humanitarian disaster looming in Africa and get on with doing what they can. But a call to arms based on the imagery of "the rest against the West" will neither help the rest nor galvanize the West.

Too Much Europe

Decisionmakers on both sides of the Atlantic appear to recognize that the West must seek to hang together because of common values and purposes, not common fears. Increasing integration within western Europe and the opening of the EU and NATO to the new democracies of central Europe are supposed to invigorate the West while erasing, not recreating, geopolitical cleavages.

Because they have mapped out futures for the EU and NATO that are far too ambitious, however, the leaders of the West are in the process of bringing about the demise of these institutions, not their revitalization. As they should, both bodies intend to take advantage of the historic opportunity to open their doors to central Europe. But they have yet to loosen their internal structures, a necessary step if their plans for enlargement are to have the intended consequences.

The EU continues to move toward a federal Europe—monetary union and a common foreign and security policy are the next steps—even as it prepares to double its membership. But the ambitious vision laid out in the Maastricht Treaty no longer enjoys even the restricted popular support that it did five years ago, when the treaty passed national referendums by the narrowest of margins.[16] Indeed, the recent Intergovernmental Conference in Turin, Italy, was primarily an exercise in damage limitation, masking the reality that national states across Europe are reasserting their sovereignty, not withering away.

Deepening European integration has lost not only its popular appeal, but also its strategic purpose. Enlargement is now the geopoliti-

---

16. In France, for example, a referendum held in September 1992 approved the Maastricht Treaty by 51.05 percent to 48.95 percent. In Denmark, a referendum rejected the treaty in June 1992. In a second vote, in May 1993, Danes approved the treaty by 56.8 percent to 43.2 percent.

cal necessity—and not just to the east. The EU's current plans for a Europe-only single market, even if good for the welfare of its member states in the short run, will likely harm the global economy in the long run. Although the North American Free Trade Agreement (NAFTA) and the Asia-Pacific Economic Cooperation (APEC) forum also aim to promote regional integration, they differ from the EU in one crucial respect: the United States links the two regions through its participation in NAFTA and membership in APEC. As trade within North America and Asia increases and becomes more liberal, so will trade between the two regions. In contrast, if the EU forged ahead on its own to build a single market, single currency, and central bank, Europe's integration into the global economy would be jeopardized. Enlargement to the east makes this drift all the more likely because the free flow of goods from central Europe will threaten producers in western Europe, generating new pressures for protection from non–EU imports. Because Europe's welfare state is more extensive and its corporate and financial structures less adaptive than their counterparts in North America, lagging competitiveness will also create incentives for the EU to put up protective barriers.[17]

A single currency is expected to help Europe climb out of its extended period of slow growth and become more competitive. And there is little doubt that the euro will bring economic benefits. The economic gains a single currency is likely to produce, however, do not alone confirm the desirability of monetary union. Precisely because political objectives have been paramount in fueling the push for a single currency, European monetary union (EMU) must be evaluated in terms of its political as well as its economic merits. After all, elected leaders looking to endow Europe with a more pronounced supranational character, not corporate leaders looking to increase profits, have been monetary union's main sponsors.

Within Europe's dominant narrative, EMU is meant to fulfill two geopolitical objectives. First, it is intended to lock in the Franco-German coalition by transferring authority over monetary policy from the national to the supranational level and by abolishing one of the most

17. For an excellent discussion of European and American industrial structures and patterns of innovation, see David Soskice, "Openness and Diversity: Thinking about Transatlantic Commercial Relations," in Barry Eichengreen, ed., *Transatlantic Economic Relations in the Post–Cold War Era* (New York: Council on Foreign Relations, 1998).

powerful symbols of sovereignty—national currencies. Second, it is supposed to create an inner core of expanding, integrated economies that will act as a magnet, drawing the EU's smaller states toward the center. A Europe of concentric circles will emerge, with successive enlargements of the inner core taking place as states not initially included in EMU meet the criteria and are able to keep pace with France, Germany, and those other EU members moving most rapidly along the path of deeper integration.

The appeal of this vision notwithstanding, it is by no means clear that a single currency will have these intended geopolitical effects. The integrity of the Franco-German coalition is, to be sure, essential to preserving an integrated, cohesive Europe. Indeed, the Paris-Bonn (soon to be Paris-Berlin) axis is the centerpiece of the European construct. It provides the EU an identifiable power center and a hierarchical structure of governance extending outward from this center. At the same time, the coalition also serves as an instrument that binds and moderates the influence of Europe's core. This dual function is what allows France and Germany to guide the EU without appearing to dominate it. Europe's smaller states are willing to enter the EU precisely because it provides reassurance that the continent's power center will exercise its influence in a moderate and benign manner.[18]

The problem is that EMU may well strain, rather than strengthen, the Franco-German coalition. Less than 40 percent of the German electorate favors currency union, largely because the deutsche mark remains a powerful symbol of national identity. Establishing a supranational monetary authority, by triggering a popular backlash against increasing integration, may well induce a reassertion of French and German sovereignty. In the same way, the economic austerity needed to meet the Maastricht criteria might lead to setbacks in the Franco-German relationship. Workers in France and Germany have already resorted to strikes to protest the cutbacks in spending implemented by their governments. Thus far elected officials in both countries have explained the need for cutbacks in terms of inefficiencies in their own economies; they have

---

18. For a more detailed exposition of the dual character of contemporary power centers, the notion of self-binding, and the application of these ideas to developments in Europe, North America, and East Asia, see Charles Kupchan, "After Pax Americana: Benign Power, Regional Integration, and the Sources of a Stable Multipolarity, *International Security*, vol. 23, no. 2 (fall 1998).

studiously avoided blaming the Maastricht criteria. But as austerity continues, exercising such restraint will prove more difficult, and both French and German elites will be tempted to blame Europe and each other for the deprivation. If the allure of political opportunism prevails, not just the single currency, but also the integrity of the Franco-German coalition, will be at risk.

Even if a common currency succeeds in locking in a prosperous and cohesive Franco-German core, the broader construction that results may well consist of concentric barriers rather than concentric circles. Monetary union will have the greatest payoffs among the advanced economies of northern Europe. Similar structures and levels of performance will maximize the benefits associated with larger economies of scale and lower transaction costs while minimizing EMU's distorting effects on national labor markets. In the economies of southern Europe, however, EMU may well cause considerable dislocation and substantial increases in unemployment because of its effect on wages.[19] EU members initially outside the inner core may therefore choose to remain where they are. Those that ultimately choose to join EMU may find that they wish they had not.

The symbolic politics of EMU will create its own barriers. In deciding to proceed with a single currency, the EU is entering a new phase in its evolution—one in which the de jure equality of its members will give way to their de jure differentiation. De jure differentiation, at least on deductive grounds, risks turning the centripetal force that has drawn Europe's periphery toward its center into a centrifugal force that will drive center and periphery apart.

Exclusion from the inner core could raise concern about relative gains, a concern that has thus far been sublimated by de jure equality. Even if the benefits of participation in the EU remained strong in absolute terms, new dividing lines might make peripheral states more sensitive to their position relative to the core.[20] EMU might also lead to relative losses in

19. See Erik Jones, "Economic and Monetary Union: Playing with Money," in Andrew Moravcsik, ed., *Centralization or Fragmentation? Europe before the Challenges of Deepening, Diversity, and Democracy* (New York: Council on Foreign Relations, 1998); and Lloyd Gruber, "Power Politics and the Transformation of European Monetary Relations," presented at the annual meeting of the American Political Science Association, San Francisco, August, 1996.

20. De jure equality, by promoting a sense of collectivity, may enable members to be concerned more with the well-being of the EU as a whole than with their own welfare. De jure differentiation, by eroding a sense of the collective, increases the likelihood that members will be more concerned about individual gain.

the periphery as the inner circle reaped the benefits of a single currency and left behind its less fortunate neighbors. Barriers could also result from the explicit relegation of some states to a second-class status, producing a sense of injury and rejection in affected states and an effort to distance themselves from the source of that injury. Finally, EMU could cause fragmentation in the construction of Europe by triggering competition among peripheral states to attain entry into the inner circle. Fearful of being left out of monetary union or other aspects of integration pursued by the core, neighboring states may vie with each other to clear the hurdles for entry, triggering both old and new rivalries.[21] At a minimum, the EU needs to think through these issues before it goes ahead with a multispeed construction, only to find that an inner circle, far from serving as the engine behind deeper integration, begins to delineate new fault lines across Europe.

Europe's wealthier states will no longer bear the cost of ensuring that the EU's poorer members stay on track. The EU has thus far been able to deepen and widen simultaneously in large part because less developed countries have been kept happy through direct financial assistance. The pie for aid is shrinking, however, even as claims on it promise to expand. Germany, for one, is unlikely to continue covering almost one-third of the EU budget. The costs of integrating eastern Germany have been enormous. High wages are forcing major German firms to move production outside the country. And daunting demographic figures loom on the horizon. By 2020, there will be one German pensioner for every German worker.[22] Come the next century, Germany will not be expending resources to ensure that its neighbors join a European currency union.

At the same time, political integration has lagged considerably behind progress on the economic front, ensuring that the Maastricht agenda will be more a mantra than a map. The EU has gone far in nurturing a European identity that sits comfortably alongside national identities. But Europeans are not, and may never be, ready to move from a fundamentally intergovernmental union to one that smacks of federalism. The hall-

21. Efforts to gain early entry into NATO have already triggered jockeying among the new democracies of central Europe. Rather than cooperating with each other on security matters, states of the region have focused almost exclusively on attaining NATO membership, showing little concern for the strategic and political implications of their admission for neighboring countries.

22. Martin Walker, "Overstretching Teutonia," *World Policy Journal*, vol. 12, no. 1 (Spring 1995).

mark of a federal system is the existence of a legitimate, representative arena of politics that operates above individual state units. The European Parliament, however, is still without real legislative authority and remains a forum for speech making, not decisionmaking. The European Commission continues to churn out proposals for increased political integration, but most have first to be approved at the national level. Even as borders become more porous, powerful cultural and linguistic dividing lines continue to fortify the national state. Opinion polls reveal that publics are at best ambivalent about further encroachments on national sovereignty, with support for a single currency hovering at about 50 percent.[23]

The Maastricht Treaty envisioned a common foreign and security policy, but the outlook on this front is bleak as well. The Western European Union (WEU), the Europe-only defense organization that has effectively lain dormant since its inception in 1948, is to develop the capability to operate independently of NATO and to extend collective defense guarantees to states that have recently joined the EU or intend to do so in the future. But if western European countries could not more fully integrate their foreign policies during the cold war, why should they be able to do so now?

In the absence of a unifying Soviet threat, the security interests of individual states are drifting apart, not coming together. Germany is far more concerned about developments in central Europe than is Spain, Portugal, or France, countries that at least for now are far more preoccupied with North Africa. The failure of the EU and NATO to take more effective and timely steps to stop the slaughter in Bosnia made clear that Europe's security is now divisible. Which EU members, for example, would today rush to defend the Finnish border against a Russian incursion, a task to which all should be committed in principle since Finland entered the EU in 1995?

The EU's notable lack of progress in forging a common foreign and defense policy stems from two main sources. First, the union continues to strive for a consensus among all its members, ensuring that it gravitates toward the lowest common denominator. Waiting for a union-wide foreign policy to emerge is a recipe for paralysis. Not until the EU is ready to act via ad hoc coalitions of the willing can it succeed in taking on more defense responsibilities. In practice, this approach means rely-

---

23. Eurobarometer, *Brussells*. March 1998.

ing more heavily on the Franco-German coalition to orchestrate collective action, enlisting the participation of other EU members on a case-by-case basis.

Second, France and Germany share less common ground on defense matters than they do on matters of economic integration. Part of the problem is the weight of history and Germany's continuing reluctance to participate fully in multilateral military operations. But French and German leaders also hold incompatible conceptions of the ultimate objectives and character of the union. For Germany, Europe is a construct for binding, moderating, and managing power—in short, for ensuring that the continent never again falls prey to the destructive forces of national rivalry. This perspective is not just a reaction against World War II. It has deep roots going back to the Holy Roman Empire, which aimed to dampen ambition and diffuse power in Europe. For France, the EU is more about amassing and projecting power, aggregating the union's military and economic resources so that it can assert itself as a global actor. The EU is to do for Europe what the national state is no longer strong enough to do for France. This perspective too has deep historical roots that trace back to Jacobin and Napoleonic conceptions of France's destiny as a great power.

Melding these competing visions of Europe will be no easy task. Germans will need to become more comfortable with leading a Europe that is more engaged and active in global affairs. The French will need to adapt their conceptions of what constitutes a more assertive Europe, choosing to apply their efforts to facilitate Europe's equal participation in broad multilateral undertakings instead of pursuing an independent course under the illusion that doing so constitutes leadership. Unless they arrive at a common conception of the broad objectives of integration, Germany and France together will be unable to provide the guidance needed to forge a coherent European defense policy.

The EU's plans for simultaneous widening make these numerous obstacles to deepening all the more formidable. Integrating the economies of the new democracies into the EU would bloat the organization's budget and pit central and southern Europe against each other in a competition for regional development funds. Because of central Europe's sizable farming sector and the common agricultural policy's price supports and export subsidies, the eastward enlargement of the union would burden the EU with enormous outlays. Swelling the EU to twice its present membership would, by complicating decisionmaking, put an end to

)

Maastricht's already unrealistic political agenda. A common foreign and security policy that would reconcile the interests of some thirty states, for example, would be out of the question.

By so overreaching, the EU opens itself up to two possible missteps of great geopolitical import. First, in light of the tradeoffs between deepening and widening, the EU's pursuit of a federal Europe comes at the expense of its eastward enlargement. The tighter the internal structures, the higher the hurdles for entry. The more energy and resources expended in deepening, the less left over for widening. Enlargement will require reform of the EU's cumbersome decisionmaking procedures, expensive agricultural subsidies, and regional development program. But to delay the inclusion of the new democracies into Europe's markets and councils while the EU pursues illusory aspirations of federalism is to miss a historic opportunity to widen the continent's zone of democracy and peace. Though less urgent, the westward enlargement of the single market to North America is equally important as a bulwark against Europe's drift from the global economy.

Second, the EU's excessive ambition could jeopardize the progress that western Europe has already made in building an integrated union of democracies at peace. The vision only dreamed of by the original architects of European integration is now a reality. Trying to do more at this juncture risks overburdening institutions and triggering a backlash among nation-states bristling at what electorates will view as both unjustified and unwanted infringements on national sovereignty. If the union continues to cling to a vision its members states will summarily reject, it will suffer irreparable damage. The EU should consolidate its achievements rather than gamble for more and risk Europe's undoing in the process.

Too Much NATO

Current plans for the enlargement of NATO are equally problematic.[24] Because NATO is a traditional military alliance whose purpose is to concentrate power against an external threat, its enlargement will as a matter of course induce Russia to marshal a countervailing coalition and will leave in strategic limbo those states left between Russia and NATO's

---

24. For citations to articles arguing for and against NATO enlargement, see chapter 2.

new eastern border. Expanding NATO in its current guise promises to resurrect, not eliminate, rivalry between Europe's east and west. Enlargement will also erode the alliance from within as current members balk at assuming new responsibilities. The days of expansive strategic interests are no longer; faced with shrinking threats, status quo powers are becoming less willing to take on defense commitments. As for ensuring American engagement in Europe, NATO enlargement promises to do just the opposite. If institutions evolve as planned, economic and security matters will still be addressed in separate bodies, leaving NATO as America's primary institutional link to Europe. But defense policy no longer enjoys a position of primacy among either electorates or their leaders, making NATO in virtually any form a weak foundation for bridging the Atlantic.

NATO must take the lead in consolidating a democratic peace in central Europe and incorporating the region into a meaningful security structure. But these tasks need not and should not entail NATO's eastward expansion as a cold war military alliance. It is the formal extension of the mutual defense provisions of Article V of the 1949 North Atlantic Treaty that promises to irk Russia and relegate those central European states not admitted to a gray zone of uncertainty. The formality and cost of treaty-based territorial guarantees also threaten to make future waves of NATO enlargement founder on the shoals of America's domestic politics.

The risks of enlarging NATO as a traditional military alliance might be justified if a major external threat to central European states arose. But Russia is neither interested in nor capable of mounting such a threat. Moscow does not protest NATO's increasing engagement in Europe's east. Russia has joined the Partnership for Peace, watched passively as NATO troops conducted exercises with local forces in Poland and the Czech Republic, sent its own troops to the United States to train with U.S. forces, and agreed in all but name to put under NATO command its soldiers enforcing the Dayton Accord in Bosnia. What Russia objects to—justifiably—is the formal enlargement of a military bloc from which it would be excluded.

Similarly, electorates in NATO countries, if they care at all, are happy to see their militaries collaborate with former adversaries. When successive waves of NATO enlargement come before the U.S. Senate, however, and the associated costs and responsibilities become apparent, the electorate will be neither apathetic nor acquiescent. Party discipline was sufficient to ensure approval of the first wave of new entrants—Poland, Hungary, and the Czech Republic.[25] But as commitments continue to expand in step with NATO's borders, and especially if some of those commitments actually come due, the process of enlargement is likely to stall. Bosnia is the best case for testing Congress's appetite for sending troops into harm's way in Europe. And Congress's reluctance to leave peacekeepers in the Balkans does not augur well for its willingness to stand behind the paper commitments entailed in expanding NATO. It is troubling, to say the least, that many members of Congress are so ready to call for America's withdrawal from Bosnia at the same time that they rally behind extending iron-clad defense guarantees to countries just north of Bosnia. Europe's new democracies would not be alone in suffering a setback if NATO legislatures reject enlargement. If NATO stakes its future on moving east, only to have its plans shot down by the public, it will itself be dealt a crippling blow.

An Atlantic Union

America belongs in Europe, and central Europe belongs in the West. But if Western leaders are to achieve these aims, they must scale back their aspirations and focus on consolidating what already exists—a peaceful, integrated community of democratic nation-states. The challenge is to find a balance between an institutional structure that demands too much, and thus falls prey to overextension, and one that delivers too little and atrophies from irrelevance. In addition, strategic matters must no longer be divorced from economic considerations. National security concerns will not remain sufficiently salient to serve as the West's binding glue. The Western democracies ultimately will hang together only if their citizens sense that they occupy a unique political community and have vested interests in seeing that community preserved. Economic and

25. On April 30, 1998, the U.S. Senate voted by a margin of 80 to 19 to admit these three countries to NATO. Public opinion polls show more ambivalence about the issue. Some 62 percent of the American public favors admitting "some Eastern European countries such as Poland, Hungary, and the Czech Republic." This figure drops to roughly 45 percent when respondents are made aware of the costs and responsibilities associated with enlargement. See "Americans on Expanding NATO," Program on International Policy Attitudes, School of Public Affairs, University of Maryland, Steven Kull, Principal Investigator, October 1, 1996.

political arguments will have to carry at least part of the weight once borne by strategic concerns.

An Atlantic union that would incorporate the EU, WEU, and NATO fulfills these criteria.[26] The initial members of the AU would be the current members of these three organizations. The AU would then expand at a steady pace not just to central Europe, but also to Russia and the other states of the former Soviet Union. The infrastructure of the EU and NATO would serve as a ready foundation for the new body. States joining the AU would take on three basic commitments: to introduce a single market, to uphold collective security, and to expand political engagement at the transnational level.

Calls for the negotiation of a free trade area encompassing North America and western Europe have already surfaced on both sides of the Atlantic. Part of the impetus comes from favorable economic prospects: the removal of remaining barriers would, by 2000, increase transatlantic trade by at least 20 percent.[27] The introduction of a single market would likely be accompanied by an investment protocol and more convergence on regulations and standards, increasing the flow of capital and prompting industrial restructuring in Europe and North America.[28] It would also help prevent both areas from drifting toward protectionism and emerging as regional trade blocs. Instead, the United States would serve as the pivot of an integrated global economy, connecting a transatlantic free trade zone with one encompassing the Pacific Rim.

The most potent appeal of the Atlantic union's single market is, however, its political significance. The conclusion of the Uruguay Round of trade negotiations reduced trade barriers in most sectors to minimum levels. And the EU and the United States agreed at their summit in Madrid in 1995 to pursue a host of follow-up measures. The elimination of re-

---

26. On the general notion of establishing a union of Atlantic democracies, see Deutsch, *Political Community and the North Atlantic Area*; and Clarence Streit, *Union Now: A Proposal for a Federal Union of the Democracies of the North Atlantic*, 8th ed. (Harper, 1939).

27. Clyde V. Prestowitz Jr., Lawrence Chimerine, and Andrew Szamosszegi, "The Case for a Transatlantic Free Trade Zone," in Bruce Stokes, ed., *Open for Business: Creating a Transatlantic Marketplace* (New York: Council on Foreign Relations, 1996), p. 22.

28. I am not suggesting that an Atlantic single market should aspire toward the same degree of standardization as a European single market, nor that the EU should relax its rules on standardization in order to attain a better fit with the North American market. Rather, both sides should strive for as much convergence as possible, while recognizing that incompatibilities will remain in certain sectors—electrical plugs and voltage, for example.

maining impediments would threaten powerful sectors such as agriculture and textiles and thus would call for heavy lifting. But just as the introduction of a single market in Europe made borders more porous, facilitated political integration, and promoted a sense of common identity, so would the creation of a single Atlantic market strengthen the underpinnings of the community of North American and European democracies. Winning congressional approval of a transatlantic free trade zone would not be easy, but a high-profile debate that connected America's prosperity to Europe's fate would drive home to Americans that they share a unique political space with Europeans.

Building an Atlantic community of strong national states that are closely integrated economically is a far more realistic enterprise than constructing a federal Europe that sublimates the national state and that omits North America from its central project. Returning to some elements of the EU's current agenda for deepening may prove expedient down the road. A single Atlantic currency, for example, is not unimaginable. But first things first. Deepening makes sense only when it will not come at the expense of the far more vital enterprise of consolidating and enlarging a stable, prosperous union of Atlantic democracies.

The Atlantic union's commitments to collective security would be looser and less automatic than NATO's current commitments to collective defense, removing the key stumbling block to a broader Western security community.[29] The AU would replace NATO's Article V guarantee and its emphasis on territorial defense with a focus on peacekeeping and peace enforcement; confronting external threats as well as those that might arise from within, it would coordinate multilateral operations across Europe. Members would affirm their intention to solve conflicts peacefully whenever possible and, when necessary, to use military force to defend against common threats. Case-by-case decisionmaking and a broad mandate to preserve peace in the Atlantic area would be the organizing principles of a new U.S.-European security bargain and a revamped NATO. Granted, the elimination of NATO's Article V guarantee

29. For discussion of the difference between collective security and collective defense see Arnold Wolfers, "Collective Defense versus Collective Security," in Arnold Wolfers, ed., *Discord and Collaboration* (Johns Hopkins University Press, 1962); and Inis Claude, *Power and International Relations* (Random House, 1962). For different interpretations of the nature of commitments to joint action under collective security, see John Mearsheimer, "The False Promise of International Institutions," *International Security*, vol. 19, no. 3 (Winter 1994/95), pp. 5–49; and Charles Kupchan and Clifford Kupchan, "The Promise of Collective Security," *International Security*, vol. 20, no. 1 (Summer 1995), pp. 52–61.

would weaken the alliance's deterrent power. But as long as Russia continues to pose no threat to central or western Europe, compromising
deterrence and holding out to Russia and its immediate neighbors a realistic prospect of inclusion in the West makes good strategic sense.

Scaling back NATO's mission and relaxing the commitments its members are expected to uphold is both a logical necessity in the absence of
an enemy and a maneuver that would circumvent many of the problems plaguing current plans for NATO's enlargement. Under the guise
of the AU, a transformed NATO could soon open its doors to all the new
democracies of central Europe without appearing anti-Russian. Defense
concerns would recede into the background; joining the AU would be
joining a civic community, not a military alliance. Collective security
commitments would provide the central Europeans some, but not all, of
the assurance they seek. American troops would stay in Europe. NATO's
existing infrastructure would remain intact. Militaries in the new democracies would continue the planning and exercising already begun
through the Partnership for Peace, furthering their integration into the
Western security community and their ability to operate with the forces
of current NATO members. But this steady integration would occur qui-
etly, avoiding the fanfare and political histrionics that promise to make
the admission of new members to today's NATO so problematic.

To be sure, these new arrangements would involve a sleight of hand.
Central Europe, via AU membership, would secure a place under the
West's protective umbrella. But couching new commitments in a broader
political context and making them more contingent on strategic circum-
stance, and thus less formal and automatic, would make central Europe's
early inclusion in the West far more palatable to Russia as well as to
electorates in NATO countries. Central European states would get to
join the club, even if that club proves to be less exclusive and selective
than the new entrants would like.

Doing away with Article V commitments also permits a broader re-
definition of Europe's boundaries. Because NATO is still a formal military alliance, only countries deemed of sufficient strategic value to
warrant their defense will ultimately be eligible for membership. Some
proponents of NATO expansion have already begun to argue that enlargement should go no further than Poland, Hungary, and the Czech
Republic, the countries that occupy the main corridor between Russia
and western Europe. But this plan leaves most of central Europe out in
the cold.

In contrast, states would join the AU as they demonstrated a commitment to democracy, markets, and international norms of behavior, offering the prospect of inclusion to all of central Europe as well as the former Soviet Union. A pan-European collective security system could become a reality, not just rhetoric to placate Russia as Poland enters a NATO that may well never extend farther east. At the same time, should Russian democracy falter, the AU's military infrastructure could serve as the foundation for a new, enlarged anti-Russian alliance.

Finally, merging NATO with the EU and WEU avoids a looming crisis over the responsibilities of these institutions. The three already have incongruent memberships that will grow only more inconsistent if they independently pursue their respective plans for enlargement. If, as in the most likely scenario, the EU and the WEU incorporate ten or more central European countries while NATO stops after accepting only a few, the United States and its main European partners will no longer share parallel strategic commitments on the continent. The AU, on the other hand, would keep American and European commitments in step, preserving the sense of common purpose that undergirds the Atlantic community.

Regardless of how far east the AU ultimately reaches, its major powers should form a directorate to prevent the sequential entry of new members from making the body unwieldy. This directorate would provide a small, flexible forum in which the major powers could forge a consensus, and it would guide the AU on both military and economic matters. The absence of a formal mechanism for great-power leadership has prevented the Organization for Security and Cooperation in Europe from fulfilling its potential. Moreover, an informal concert of major states already calls the shots on the continent. The Contact Group formed to seek a settlement in Bosnia comprised the United States, Germany, France, Britain, and Russia. In practice, both NATO and the EU function by fashioning agreement among their leading members. A major power directorate at the core of the AU would only formalize present realities, while making possible effective decisionmaking and timely collective action.

The final pillar of an Atlantic union is deepened civic engagement on the transnational level.[30] Civic society among nation-states emerges from

---

30. For discussion of civic engagement within and among the members of the Atlantic community, see Josef Janning, Charles Kupchan, and Dirk Rumberg, eds., *Civic Engagement in the Atlantic Community* (Gutersloh: Bertelsmann Foundation, 1998).

political participation and community association, just as it does within nation-states. If the Atlantic community is to survive and prosper, its citizens must share a sense of belonging not only to their national states, but also to a transnational political space that the Western democracies inhabit. The legitimacy that the institutions of the EU enjoy in member states, for instance, is not just a function of the services they provide. It is also a reflection of the degree to which Europe has come to compete with the nation-state as a defining element of individual identity and allegiance.

The cold war bequeathed to the West a rich network of public institutions and associations as well as private enterprises and groups that transcend national boundaries. Thickening this network so that it becomes the enduring social and political fabric of an Atlantic union entails several tasks. The European Parliament should be enlarged into an Atlantic parliament and charged with providing legislative oversight of the AU. National parliaments would retain the lion's share of legislative authority, but handing over a substantive portfolio of responsibilities to an Atlantic parliament would nurture a Western political identity that complements national loyalties, thereby legitimating a transatlantic polity. The Atlantic parliament's duties would include designing the AU's budget, aligning American and European social policies, and developing union-wide laws and regulations.

Public and private groups should ensure the flowering of the many forms of transatlantic association—business contacts, religious and cultural activities, social causes, and leisure activities. These associations will intensify citizens' engagement in and identification with a transatlantic polity. Educational and vocational exchanges and scientific and industrial collaboration should also be promoted. Finally, Western governments should launch ambitious education campaigns to inform their electorates of the importance of public engagement in preserving and widening the transatlantic community. The West is at risk in part because it lacks the defining images and projects that galvanize domestic polities. Constructing an Atlantic union of democracies will not call up the same sense of collective commitment and sacrifice as the struggle against communism. Yet it need not. Bold leadership in laying out a vision of a peaceful, prosperous union of Atlantic democracies and proceeding with the necessary institutional innovations will suffice to wean citizens away from domestic preoccupations and inspire them to construct a new West.

A Conservative Revolution

Constructing an Atlantic union is not just a prudential move aimed at making permanent the historic transformation of the Atlantic area from a zone of war into a zone of peace. It would also lay the groundwork for a more integrated and cooperative global order. To make the renovation of the West a top priority of U.S. foreign policy is not to demote other regions or indicate that the Western democracies must prepare to do battle against them. On the contrary, locking in peaceful relations among the Atlantic democracies will free the Western powers to address challenges elsewhere. A strong Atlantic coalition will also increase the West's leverage in other regions. As they work to build an Atlantic union, the United States and EU members should explicitly seek to augment cooperation with powers outside the Atlantic area and help promote stability in those areas. Although its results were less substantive than symbolic, the EU-Asia summit in Bangkok in 1996 was an important step in the right direction.

While strengthening its ties to other regions, the AU should also foster regional integration elsewhere. Linked by global trade and coordination among the great powers, regional unions along the AU model in Asia and Africa could eventually consolidate new zones of peace and provide the foundation for a more stable international order. The main reason for not inviting Japan, one of Asia's most democratic and prosperous nations, to join the AU is that a focus on the Atlantic community would distract Japan from facilitating further integration in its own neighborhood. The AU is thus the first step toward the creation of a global concert of democratic great powers that would coordinate relations among and within regional organizations.

The AU would also serve as the driving force behind the liberalization of global trade. Through successive accessions to NAFTA, a transatlantic free trade zone would gradually extend throughout Central and South America. Because the EU is already looking south as well as east, an Atlantic single market might eventually include the Middle East and North Africa. Fearful of being excluded from the AU's widening trade zone, other areas would face pressure to open their own markets in return for access. The geoeconomic move toward globalization would balance the geopolitical move toward regionalization.

Constructing an Atlantic union is a conservative enterprise. Plans that call for further sacrifices and increased responsibilities, like monetary union and NATO expansion, have little public appeal in this era of waning internationalism. A more modest set of objectives is needed to fashion a new consensus. Rather than deepening institutions, the AU would extend their reach, reasonably asking electorates on both sides of the Atlantic to form a single market, uphold collective security, and send representatives to a common parliament. By solidifying a transatlantic community at peace, an Atlantic union would do much more for the West and the rest of the world than monetary union in Europe or tank traps on the Poland-Belarus border. If the AU successfully consolidates the democratic peace, what appears mundane today will, in the longer course of history, prove revolutionary.[31]

31. An earlier version of this essay appeared as "Reviving the West," *Foreign Affairs,* vol. 75, no. 3 (May/June 1996).

About the Authors

Charles A. Kupchan
Senior Fellow at the Council on Foreign Relations and Professor of International Relations at Georgetown University

Stephen M. Walt
Professor of Political Science and Master of the Social Sciences Collegiate Division at the University of Chicago

Ole Wæver
Senior Research Fellow at the Copenhagen Peace Research Institute and lecturer at the Institute of Political Science, University of Copenhagen